THE RELATION OF THE BIBLE

TO LEARNING

The Relation of the Bible to Learning

by

H. Evan Runner

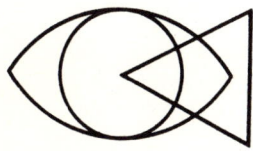

wedge publishing foundation

Post office box 10, Station L/Toronto 10, Ontario, Canada

Third edition

Copyright Canada 1970 © Wedge Publishing Foundation

All rights reserved. No part of this book may be reproduced in any form without permission in writing from the publishers.

Preface

The chapters of this volume represent two series of lectures, of which those reproduced in the introduction and in the first three chapters were given in 1959 and those in the last two a year later. Both series were on the program of the first two years of study conferences held at Unionville, Ontario, under the auspices of the Association for Reformed Scientific Studies. Even though the material here presented was not originally given all in one piece, the bundling of the lectures does provide the reader with a more comprehensive view of the issues at stake and with an integral continuity in direction. As such the pages of this book are all of one piece.

The original audiences of the Unionville conferences consisted, to a much greater degree than has become the case later, largely of young christian students who had more or less recently immigrated from the Netherlands to Canada. This has somewhat affected the form of the lectures, since they were in part adapted to fit their peculiar circumstances. Nevertheless, the underlying themes and issues rise above and beyond the particular shape in which they were presented and claim a universal validity for themselves. As, indeed, they presented themselves to the author who, though himself an American from Scotch-Irish extraction, had become impressed with the importance of work done in the Netherlands during the course of theological and philosophical studies.

The central and most crucial issues in these lectures arise from an altogether vitally concerned struggle with the alleged autonomy of matters academic. One hears everywhere today that there is no intrinsic connection between the Word of God and our scientific or scholarly pursuits. And even if such a connection be at times confessed with the lips, the scientific activities of the speaker more often than not proclaim a conviction rooted in a lack of such a connection. These lectures spring forth from the conviction that the Word of God as "Orderer" of all creation addresses itself to the totality of human experience, as the supremely authoritative condition for all meaningful experience, as both the limit and the source of all meaning. The place of scholarly activity as one human task among many in the integral unity of life presupposes that all things academic depend on subjection to the Word for their meaning.

CONTENTS

	Page
Introduction	11

Lecture I
Thesis ... 21

Lecture II
Antithesis ... 35

Lecture III
Synthesis ... 63

Lecture IV
Scientific and Pre-Scientific ... 87

Lecture V
Sphere-Sovereignty ... 131

The author

Dr. H. Evan Runner was born at Oxford, Pennsylvania, and graduated from Wheaton College, Illinois, in 1936. Since then he has pursued studies at Westminster Theological Seminary in Philadelphia, the Theological School of the Reformed Churches in The Netherlands, and the Divinity School of Harvard University. From 1941 to 1943 he was a Junior Fellow of the Society of Fellows of Harvard University. In 1951 he was granted the degree of Doctor of Philosophy *cum laude* by the Free University of Amsterdam upon submitting a thesis on *The Development of Aristotle Illustrated from the Earliest Books of Physics*.

Dr. Runner has taught Latin, Greek, English and History in both public and private school systems. He is well known as lecturer in the United States and Canada and has published a number of articles. Since 1959 he has taught in the Philosophy Department of Calvin College, Grand Rapids, Michigan, where at present he is full professor.

Introduction

Young people of the Reformation in Canada, I am happy to participate in this first Student Conference sponsored by the Association for Reformed Scientific Studies.* I hope today and the two days following to present three lectures entitled: Thesis, Antithesis, and Synthesis. In the lecture of Prof. Farris this morning you heard something about the use that was made of these three words by the great German philosopher Hegel. I shall not be using the words in Hegel's sense, but that will become clear as the lectures proceed.[1] In the meantime it will, I think, help you to follow and hold on to the sense of my remarks if you will keep in mind this triad: thesis—antithesis—synthesis.

Purpose of the Conference

This Study Conference, that we are just now beginning to enjoy, is designed to give the more studious and concerned among you Reformed young people in Canada a special opportunity to reflect on your distinctive calling in the world of scholarship and in society, to offer you insights that will help you while you are possibly in attendance at colleges and universities, technical and professional schools in Canada where the light, the revealing light, of the Word of God is withheld from whatever work you are there engaged in. It is also our purpose to call attention to the really desperate need that exists here in Canada for *a centre of scholarly research and university instruction of our own*, where

---

[1] For the very important difference between religious and analytical dialectic, antithesis and synthesis, see Dooyeweerd, *Vernieuwing en Bezinning*, pp. 10-13.

* Since 1959 the name has been changed to: Association for the Advancement of Christian Scholarship (A.A.C.S.)

we can, above all, just *be ourselves,* where, I mean to say, we can quite naturally and happily go from Scripture to our field of research and back again, glorying in our God and Father, Who is above all and blessed forever.

The Question

And now I shall not waste any of the precious moments at my disposal, but—in accordance with the injunction found in Ecclesiastes 9:10—plunge at once into the heart of the problem assigned to me, viz. *the relation of Scripture to learning.*

The relation of the Word of God to learning—there you have what I do not hesitate to call *the most important question the Christian student can put to himself.* In its very nature the problem is one that will *always* be of the most fundamental importance. But in a special way it presses with insistence and urgency upon *us here* at this still early stage of the emigration from the Netherlands. It is part of a larger question: *the relation of the Word of God to our life-in-the-world.* In this broader form it is THE *question of the emigration.* And if your emigration forces you in a new and living way to give (scriptural) account of *this relation,* then we can look forward to a promising future.

Ambiguity and Conflict

After you have emigrated to Canada or the U.S.A. (or, I might just as well add, to Australia or New Zealand) you discover to your dismay that the *term* Calvinism does not always stand for the same *thing;* you come to find out that Dutch Calvinism—the term is an unfortunate one, and ought to mean, if used at all, simply the revival of Biblical religion that occurred during the course of the 19th and 20th centuries in the Netherlands—that Dutch Calvinism (so understood) and the Calvinism you encounter in limited circles of the (predominantly) Anglo-Saxon civilizations are not one and the same thing. The difference can and does give rise to conflicts, *serious* conflicts. *And your generation is historically called upon to resolve the clash.* Much trouble and spiritual decline all along the line could come from a well-intentioned but ill-informed attempt, or better, *series* of attempts at resolution.

Conflicting Attempts at Resolution

Already, the growing awareness of the conflict has brought some measure of disunity into our ranks. Some would seem to have fallen victim to the blood and soil—or, seeing the make-up of your old homeland, perhaps I'd better speak of blood and soil *and water*—doctrine that Dutch Calvinism in some unexplained way is attached to life-forms exclusive to that area of the world's surface. These persons are in the process of giving in to a kind of relativism, and are farther along the road to spiritual impotence than they themselves perhaps realize.[1] Others attempt by a. compromising give-and-take to harmonize the conflicts that arise, *but without really penetrating to the real cause of the conflicts.* Like the doctor who can so often only treat symptoms, they never know what is going to happen next, and, since the disease they are dealing with is such a virulent one, they will be confronted with one crisis after another until in the end they stand in the presence of death. Still others, often called extremists or fanatics by representatives of the first two groups, feel somehow —and by "feel" here I mean not a merely psychical feeling, but rather a central-religious or prophetic discernment (what an older generation would no doubt have called *"Gereformeerde voelhoorns")*—that the difference between the two forms of Calvinism calls for decision. No relativism. No piece by piece surrender by accommodation to the new ways (sometimes euphemistically called the process of inevitable adjustment by those who do not "see" in faith the things hoped for). But *radical choice,* based on prophetic insight. To choose a different way to go does not necessarily mean isolation from persons of another 'way'. It allows for the greatest possible personal contact. By "in ons isolement ligt onze kracht" Groen van Prinsterer did not mean that we must separate ourselves from *persons,* but that in all our contacts with them we must be vividly aware of the distinctiveness of the *rule* by which our lives are directed.

'Principle' Governs Attempts at Resolution

We cannot here, of course, go into the question in its wider form. I only wish to point out that at the bottom of the differ-

---

[1] See *Christian Perspectives* 1962, p. 249 f.

ence between the various things called by the name of Calvinism, and consequently also at the bottom of the various attitudes assumed towards that difference, at the very rock bottom of all of this there lurks the question we have to deal with, the question of *the relation of Holy Scripture to our life-in-the-world*. If you have been following me so far you can see that we are here dealing with *fundamentals*.

Putting the matter quite simply, we can say that our question is the question about the meaning of Psalm 119:105: "Thy word is a lamp unto my feet, and light to my path." In yet another formulation our question is the question of *principles*. Now I know that in the Netherlands an earlier generation may sometimes have overworked the idea of principles, and also that at times perhaps the question of principles, Reformed principles—*"de Gereformeerde beginselen"*, they were called—was talked about *too abstractly*. And I am very much aware that the positivistic atmosphere of many of our Anglo-Saxon universities with its vaunted ideal of "objective" factuality works confusingly upon the Christian immigrant student at this point. But the question of principles is after all simply the question whether the Bible is a *norm,* a regulative rule (Latin, *regula)* for our living, whether it gives a *direction* to our living in this world, whether it directs us how to go, in what *way* to go. The Presbyterians among us will recall that the second question of the Westminster Shorter Catechism asks, "What rule hath God given to direct us how we may glorify and enjoy him?" And the answer follows: "The word of God, which is contained in the Scriptures of the Old and New Testaments, is the only rule to direct us how we may glorify and enjoy him." That's it. That is the answer to the question whether our life is governed by principles. And that is why it is simply impossible to avoid the *principial* question by an appeal to the "practical" bent of your Canadian neighbours. For the Word of the living God *has come* with its revealing light into our life, and *all human life,* whether men are aware of it or not, *is some kind of response to that Word*. Practice must therefore always derive from principle, although awareness of its principial origin—e.g. in a life-practice that has become a dead tradition—may grow vague with the passage of time. That is to say, *practice always derives from a way of "seeing" your life that you take to be normative.* In all practice there is present some kind of acknowledgment of an Order or Structure of things. It is this fact, and this fact alone, that makes for the high seriousness of the life-situation of you Reformation youth, the first generation of Dutch Calvinists in Canada. If you give yourselves whole-heartedly to its consideration you will undoubtedly become men, big men, *men of God*, walking with the greats of Hebrews 11. Here is all the human worth that the humanist strives to achieve in vain because he "sees" the structure of life wrongly, because he is guided by a wrong *principle*, because his life is not directed by the revealing light of the Word of God.

Our Problem Posed for the World of Learning: Two 'Ways'

The life of the student is but a part of human life in general, so that the question of the relation of the Word of God to learning is simply part of the broader question. Nevertheless, the more restricted area has some difficulties of its own, and for us who are students those difficulties are real hurdles that must be got over. To most of us, at least at first glance, the principles of mathematics and logic, for example, would very much seem to remain the same, whether Scripture is brought into the picture or not. The statement 2+2=4 is true for everybody, is it not? And thermodynamics would seem to remain thermodynamics; and agronomy, agronomy. What in the wide world then might the relation of Scripture to these and other areas of learning be? The very thought tends to make many persons think of any talk of a *Christian* cultivation of the several fields of learning as downright obscurantism and plain hypocrisy. Can one ever really speak of an *intrinsic connection* between the Word of God and the world of learning?

I spoke purposely of an *intrinsic* connection. We can all understand that you can have a Christian *man* to teach biology, or chemistry, or philosophy. But that is not the question. That could be a merely extrinsic connection. I recall that when a few years ago, after a member of the Gereformeerde Kerken had been appointed professor of philosophy at one of the state universities in the Netherlands, some Christian parents in the province involved began to ask in public whether it would henceforth be necessary to send those of their children who wished to study philosophy all the way to Amsterdam to the Free University, Professor Vollenhoven wrote very simply about it that those parents would have to learn to distinguish between a Christian man teaching philosophy and the teaching of a Christian or Scriptural philosophy. And he meant by it that the matter of supreme importance is whether the man who in his personal faith is Christian has learned through and in that faith *to see the problems of his field of study in the revealing light of the Word of God.*

That brings us back to our question, whether there is an *intrinsic* connection between the Word of God and the world of learning. Can we sincerely speak of *Scriptural* principles here? Is Scripture also in this area of our life a lamp to our feet and light to our path? If we cannot honestly answer these questions in the affirmative then we are left with merely Christian *people* who work at *a science.* A science, presumably, that has principles of its own, which secrets it yields up to those who go to work on it. An *autonomous science* (from Greek *auto, nomos,* i.e. itself its law, a law to itself), as we are accustomed to speak of it. But if *that* is the true state of affairs it *does indeed involve a different conception of the Word of God and of the Christian religion.* For there is then one area, at least, in our human life for which the Word of God gives no light, and indeed which itself *requires* no such light inasmuch as it would seem to have *a light of its own* (its own principle), *at which we can get unaided.* (The idea of the older metaphysics, of a science of a Being that exists in itself and has a—noetic—light of its own.) Then the Christian religion would have a limited validity and would have to agree with, be accommodated to, that other light of science.

The 'Way' Based on Relevancy

We have now perhaps reached the place where we can sum up our impression of the significance of the question with which we are to deal in these lectures. We can say at once that it has become evident that our question is nothing less than the *Place of the Great Decision.* Our question constitutes the *Great Divide,* the *Watershed* of our future course as Dutch immigrant students of Reformation Christianity in Canada. For if the Word of God has real relevancy to the world of learning itself, in the sense that it brings a definite *direction* into our work there that makes talk of a *Christian cultivation of learning* (i.e. "Christelijke wetenschapsbeoefening") not just so much idle, even hypocritical, chatter of old greybeards but *a matter of paramount concern for the rendering effective of Christ's redemption in that life of the Creation,* then it will be that directing faith that gathers us into a fellowship. And whatever our relations to others who, in other spirits, work in the same areas as we, our concern to understand the significance of the Word for our field of study will attach us first to other students of the same conviction of faith. Since, as we shall have occasion to see, all fields of learning constitute an organic whole, and only in organic connection can we hope to attain the proper results in our work, this fellowship in our conviction of faith will require a *scholarly community* of our own in Canada, *a fellowship of faith that pertains to the world of learning* (i.e. een geloofsgemeenschap *in academicis*). This scholarly community, which at the same time would be a fellowship of faith, would then be a configuration (i.e. *gestalte*) in the developing Kingdom of God, the Body of Christ. Faith will have assumed a visible shape or pattern.

The 'Way' Based on Denial of Relevancy

But if the relation of the Word of God to the life of learning is only of the nature of an appendix or adjunct, of an extra or added something, a *donum superadditum*, for instance; well, then, of course, we are free to follow the easier course of adaptation, of adjustment, of accommodation to the world of culture that is the product of the last centuries of modern western man's cultural labors, the world that we find in our Canadian surroundings. But then it will not be the faith that unites us in a fellowship in our academic work, but rather the work in which we are engaged as scholars. Then we shall, each for each, be busied with whatever light our fields are pleased to surrender to us. Our ultimate loyalty in our work will now be to the profession itself, to the *mind* or method of our profession. The one will be busy to take on the "mind" of the philologist; another, the "mind" of the lawyer; yet another, the "mind" of the engineer; and still another, the "mind" that is concerned, say, with the Hebrew Old Testament (and its world). Here our loyalty, in our respective fields of learning, will not be to God's Kingdom of Righteousness. Unless of course, all men who "seek the truth" are by that very fact engaged in God's Kingdom of Righteousness. But that cannot be; that is certainly in conflict with the Scriptural idea. For *Christ* is our Righteousness, and the Kingdom of Righteousness exists only where in Him, through the renewing operation of God's Holy Spirit, men have come to love the Truth as it is in Jesus, the Lord.

If God's Word therefore has no *intrinsic* connection with the world of learning, we shall never have the exhilarating joy of working together as members of Christ's Body to bring to manifestation *in our studies* patterns of God's glorious Kingdom. Left to us then is only to fall, as so many *distinct individuals*—centres of rationality, perhaps?—, into the existing programs of the several secular universities, professional and technical schools. ("Secular" here means just exactly that science shines by its own light and thus has no need of any supposed light of faith.) In the wider sense of our question it means that we are left to fall into the prevailing order and practice—except, of course, where that is too glaringly immoral, or unjust, or ugly, etc.!—of Canadian society with all its implementing agencies, and to do it, if we would not be fools, with all possible dispatch. The spirit that informs modern western society, Canadian society, will then come over us.

Each 'Way' Demands Whole of Life

Let us not comfort ourselves by saying that our Reformed Churches, our youth societies, etc. will yet be left to us. If in our search for truth we put our confidence in our "Reason" and the subjection of all things to the rational inquiry of men, we have changed entirely, as *men*. At first we may *for a time* be able to hold on to some division of our life into what historically have been called the areas of faith and of reason. But life is integral; it is all one piece. And sooner or later we shall, if we are straightforward and do not, through failure to face reality, become stunted in our growth, have to face up to the decision whether *Christ's Kingdom* is a matter of the totality of our life, or the *Kingdom of Reason*. Whether the reality of our world is rooted in the heart of man, who, standing in Christ the Redeemer, is to render obedience to the Sovereign and who has his great reward in thus keeping God's Law, or whether reality is simply something that is just there, having in it some capacity to be searched out by a Light of Reason that is just there. Both are faiths men live by. But all faith is totalitarian. And sooner or later the one will destroy the other.

The Decision

Let us make no bones about it: before us, as before Herakles, two ways lie and we must decide which one we will take, the way of accommodation to the present patterns of our world, i.e. the *Way of Synthesis,* or the *Way of Antithesis.* Again let me remind you of what I said about Groen van Prinsterer's "In ons isolement ligt onze kracht". The Antithesis is not to be taken in a subjectivistic sense, as though *I* am different from *him;* it is not some static division of society into Christian and anti-Christian groups or segments of the populace. Rather, the Antithesis is the difference of response to the Word of God, which, coming into the world as a *revealing light* for our life (Ps. 119:105), effectuates with the sovereignty of its Divine Author an abiding line of division between ways obedient and disobedient (cf. Psalm 1; Prov. 1 and 2).

Synthesis, or Antithesis? Lo, what issues hang in the balance! I can scarcely refrain from attempting a look into the future. What kind of a Canada will emerge? What will be the nature of her institutions? What direction will her Common Law take? In what channels will her scientific investigations run? And will there be everywhere only the dead uniformity of secular rationalism, or will there have grown the realistic recognition of the *role of principles in all our human life,* and of the undeniable fact that we do not all follow the same Lord, are not all directed by the same Rule (Word)?

But no more of this. In this sense the future is not "clear". There is, as yet, no future Canada. Of this one thing we can all be very sure: *the kind of Canadian society that will emerge will depend largely on you, the Reformation youth of Canada, and on the answer you give to the question I have just described as the Great Divide.*

Lecture I

Thesis

Thus far we have stated two possible attitudes towards the question as to the intrinsic connection between the Word of God and the world of learning. Now I should like to add that it would seem clear that our choice between them will depend, does depend on *what the Word of God actually is*. Whatever uncertainty there may yet be among us on the matter will undoubtedly be due to our not being sufficiently clear as to the nature of the Word of God and as to the role it must play in our life. The first question, therefore, to which I wish to address myself in these lectures is the question as to the nature and role of the Word of God.

The Crux of Our Problem

What, after all, is the Word of God? It may at first strike you as strange that this question has to be asked, particularly in our circles. Was the Protestant Reformation not first of all a rediscovery of the meaning of the Word of God? And are we not all agreed as to the meaning of that Word? I believe, however, that further reflection will convince all of us that we are here at the heart of our problem and of the cause of whatever dividedness there may be as to how we should go. I think that we shall find that for various reasons—including the too great prominence that has been given even in the history of the Reformed Churches to theology at the expense of the prophetic task that each believer has as *man* to understand the Divine Word—even we Christians of the Reformation very frequently have an inadequate understanding of the Word of God.

Word and Words

To be sure, we are familiar with this *book*, the Bible or the Holy Scriptures, a collection of sixty-six books written by many authors to whom the Word of the Lord came in divers ways. But to know about this *diversity of fact* is not in itself to know the Word of God. Among my old "fundamentalist" friends there were those who could tell you at the drop of a hat how many chapters, even verses, nay, even *words* there are in this collection of sixty-six books (at least in the King James Version!). Yet that is not in itself a knowledge of the Word of God. I know many persons who can tell you in the space of a lightning flash where a certain expression is to be found, chapter and verse. Now we certainly need also in this way to be thoroughly acquainted with the Bible, but even such knowledge is not yet the required knowledge of the Word of God. I have known people, converted in evangelistic meetings, who are at once instructed in so-called methods of personal evangelism, i.e. in ways of handling particular Bible verses to meet various types of objection to the call for a complete "surrender" to Christ. Now I would not for a moment want to disparage the learning of specific Bible verses and their use in soul-winning. In our present discussion I only mean to say that such acquaintance with diverse parts and moments of the Scriptures is not *by itself* the knowledge of the Word of God that we must have. It has been pointed out that it was of the experts in the Jewish law, the "nomikoi", that Jesus said (Luke 11:52): "Ye have taken away the key of knowledge." It is thus possible to be very much at home in the details of the Scriptures and not to know the Word of God.

The Unity of the Word

For the Word of God is *one*. Underlying all the diversity of the Scriptures as we have them in this temporal life is the unity of the Word of God. It is, after all, the WORD. How else could this big collection of sixty-six books be properly spoken of as the Word? And whence the "system" of systematic or dogmatic theology? It is not the mind of the theologian, going to work on the many texts of Scripture, that constructs for the first time out of many passages a unity of meaning. This unity the theologian does not *make;* he *finds* it. The Divine Word *is* one, and *as such* is the POWER, living and active, that pierces to the heart and converts the soul (Rom. 1:16; Hebr. 4:12; Ps. 19:7; James 1:18; cf. I Cor. 1:18, 24). In the very first place it is not we who come with our understanding to the Word of God (taken, for example, in the sense of the collection of many logical judgments or, if you will, propositions making up our Scriptures), but it is the WORD, which is the POWER of God, that comes to our hearts and opens our eyes so that we may understand the singleness of meaning of all the many Scriptures. This Word comes to us not as theologians but as men and directs all our life-activities, including those we call theological. Our knowledge of the Word does not come from the application of a grammatical-historical exegetical method. For a man can read the Scriptures with a *covering* before his eyes. (II Cor. 3:14-16) In our exegesis or effort at getting at the meaning of this or that passage of the Bible *the Word is or is not already at work.* God is first with our souls, also here, and there is no sure ground for our lives in our methods. The Word of God is the only firm foundation of our life. A *proper* understanding of the Scriptures is only possible when we are *already* in the grip of the Word, the active, renewing Word of God.

Just as the Scriptures are the Word of God written, so Christ is the Word of God come in the flesh. For that reason we may say that *Christ* is the meaning, the unity of the Scriptures. Thus we read of Philip's encounter with the Ethiopian eunuch that "beginning at the same scripture"—viz. Isaiah 53—"he preached unto him Jesus." When however we say that Christ is the meaning of the Scriptures, we must know *what* we are saying. In a moment I shall come back to this matter of the unity of the Word of God. But first let me suggest a number of ways in which our own Reformed practices may work to hinder our understanding of it.

Hindering Factors

Take, for example, our *family devotions*. In the American fundamentalist circles in which I was brought up personal reading of the Bible was very much encouraged, but Scripture reading in the family circle at mealtime was next to unknown, at least in the actual practice. When I first became acquainted with the latter practice I was very much impressed with it. And I must say that I still feel that it is a most important factor in a Christian family life. (We are not just a collection, an aggregate of individuals!) But this, I think, ought also to be said, that if the reading at table is merely of a few verses out of a chapter, to be followed the next day by the following few verses, and if there is no *connecting comment,* and no other Bible reading being done —as I fear is frequently the case—then it is scarcely to be wondered at that we do not know the Scriptures as a single Word. For where are we ever confronted with such a Word?

Or again, take our methods of *catechizing.* How often do we get lost in subdivisions of subdivisions? Do we *place* the lesson for the day in a wider perspective? When are all the "parts" brought together to reinforce in our consciousness the *unity* of the Word?

Perhaps most important of all here is the practice of *preaching* in our churches. In how many of the sermons preached in our pulpits are we confronted with the Word, and not merely with some of the words of the Word? To be specific, what, after all, is wrong with taking some Biblical person, say Peter, and analyzing for the congregation his good and bad qualities, thus with *moralizing* sermons? What is wrong with preaching on lessons to be learned from incidents in the life of Christ, with delivering a homily on the virtue of love in I Cor. 13 taken out of all connection with the totality of Scripture and the history of redemption? Is not the evil in all these instances that we have failed to keep our eyes fixed upon the *unity of the Word?*

The point is important enough to take the time to offer you two examples of what I mean from sermons preached within the last year in Christian Reformed pulpits. One sermon dealt with the story of Elisha's healing Naaman of his leprosy (II Kings 5), and there were six points: (1) Rich men as well as poor men have their troubles (the leprosy of Naaman); (2) Big results come from small things (the little Israelitish servant girl succeeded in having the rich man of Syria go to the King of Israel); (3) Young people should study religion (the servant-girl was acquainted with the man of God, Elisha, and his miracles); (4) Knowledge is of value when it's put to practical use (the servant-girl *knew* the prophet was in Israel, but she *also thought to mention it at the proper moment*); (5) Men sometimes apply for help to the wrong sources (Naaman went to the King instead of to the prophet, to the government instead of to the Church); and— finally!—(6) The messages of God are appointed to show to men the way of salvation (Naaman is carried from healing to Healing). There you have the sermon. Now let me ask you in all seriousness, precisely how did this sermon direct the congregation to the meaning of II Kings 5 in the Divine Word? How can congregations that are subjected to such "preaching" know the *Word of God?*

The second sermon is in many ways better than the first, but on the *point at issue* perhaps no different. The sermon was based on Jeremiah 29. The Jews had at last been carried away by Nebuchadnezzar to Babylon—even the king, the queen and the court. And now Jeremiah is instructed by "the Lord of hosts, the God of Israel" to send a letter to "those whom I have caused to be carried away from Jerusalem unto Babylon". Here the people of God's choice, because of their continuing disobedience and hardness of heart, have at last experienced the wrath of the sovereign God Who had made the covenant with them. Now they are driven from the land of promise, dispersed among the heathen. Is this the final abandonment? Is this the meaning of all the promises to Abraham, to Isaac and Jacob? Is this the nature of Jehovah? What could their God have to say to them *now*? To hear the message is to be still from amazement. "Build ye houses, and dwell in them; and plant gardens, and eat the fruit of them. Take ye wives, and beget sons and daughters; and take wives for your sons, and give your daughters to husbands, that they may bear sons and daughters, that ye may be increased there, and not diminished . . . For after seventy years be accomplished at Babylon I will visit you, and perform my good word toward you, in causing you to return to this place. For I know the thoughts that I think toward you, . . thoughts of peace, and not of evil, to give you hope in your latter end. Then shall ye call upon me, and ye shall go and pray unto me, and I will hearken unto you. And (vs. 13) ye shall seek me, and find me, when ye shall search for me with all your heart. And I will be found of you, . . and turn away your captivity, and . . . gather you from all the nations . . ."

What is the Word of God here but a revelation of God's faithfulness in *this* critical portion of history to His sovereignly-given covenant-word? Yet the sermon took the words of vs. 13 *out of their context* and dealt with "Prayer in the Life of the Christian". The context of vs. 13 was simply used as *illustrative material* for a *general truth*. I suppose that just about everything that was said in the sermon was in its way scriptural. But was this sermon *preaching the Word in these words?* I dare to say, No. The text was dealt with abstractly (that is, torn out of its place) and not concretely. But then our final verdict must be that the *Word at this place in the Scriptures* was not preached. And I believe that all such preaching, for all its remaining good qualities, is essentially unsound, and does not build up in the congregation a rich and meaningful knowledge of the *Word* of God.

The One Word of God

Well, we have seen now some practices that hinder our coming to know the Word of God in its *unity*. We must return to our main point, that the Word *is* such a unity. Is it possible to make clearer, and perhaps more vivid, what we mean by this unity of the Word? I think that it is. But it will take a little time to do it.

The Word of God—the POWER we have been talking about —works in us a true knowledge of God, of our own selves and of the Law-order of God (the world-order). But these three "knowledges" are not three pieces of knowledge quite independent of each other; they are *related*.

God and Law.

Take, for instance, our knowledge of God and our knowledge of the Law. I should explain that by Law here I do not merely mean the Ten Commandments, the concentrated religious meaning of which Christ expressed in the words "Thou shalt love the Lord thy God with all thy heart, and with all thy soul, and with all thy mind . . . and thy neighbour as thyself". In addition to this religious law for the central heart-life of man I mean all those law-words of God that hold for the various aspects of persons and things, and of which we become aware in the actual living of our lives: mathematical laws, physical laws, laws for organic growth, laws of thought, economic and aesthetic laws, etc. We become aware of these laws as a binding or limiting force in our lives, as a force that holds for us and norms our lives: we do something; then we feel that it was not "good" and we draw back. In short, I mean by Law every word of God by which He has subjected the creation to His Will or Rule. Law is thus nothing other than the Will of the sovereign God for His creation. But for that very reason it is not possible to have a true knowledge of the Law apart from a true knowledge of God as sovereign Creator.

Think of the Greeks. As pagans they knew no sovereign God. Whatever gods they did acknowledge were thought of as subject to a more ultimate law of Necessity which they called *"Anangke"*. Thus in their conception Law had become *abstract*, i.e. torn from its place in a larger context or structure. It was *just simply there*, some necessary force that determines everything. Being abstract, it has become absolutized. In the realistic philosophy of Plato such absolute, abstract law-essences—e.g. 'the beautiful itself', 'the just itself', etc.—hold for the gods as well as for men. Such an absolutization of the Law at the expense of God is but one of the many distortions of the Truth that are characteristic of man in apostasy.

Unfortunately, this abstract, pagan way of conceiving the Law was adopted by many philosophers of the so-called Christian Middle Ages. We hear of the Law of Reason (!) and of Natural (!) Law. The radical departure from it that we meet in William of Occam is not a return to a scriptural view of Law. For Occam God and Law are irreconcilables. Law implies universals; Occam was a nominalist, and for nominalism only individual things really *(i.e., in re)* exist. Law therefore can only be *individual decisions* of God's Will. If God is to be free He cannot be related to any universally binding Law. God is ex-lex, Deus Exlex. There can be no universally valid moral law to which God is subject.

Calvin puts us on the track of a scriptural conception of Law when he: 1) criticizes Augustine's theory of ideas (those are that abstract Law of Platonic realism, which in the intervening period between Plato and Augustine had been subjectivized, i.e. declared to be the *a priori* equipment of Reason, thus an abstract Law now attached to our own human subjectivity as its *a priori* part) by saying that God is not bound by any Law, but 2) at the same time rejects the Occamist view of the *Deus Exlex* and points to the scriptural account of God as *faithful*. In Calvin the sovereignty of God is never conceived apart from His righteousness (justitia). Calvin teaches that God by nature loves righteousness and justice. And that is simply his way of giving expression to the scriptural idea that God puts the Law to the creation and faithfully maintains it.

By now it ought to have become clear to you that a scriptural view of the Law is intimately tied up with a scriptural view of the Divine Law-Giver. Law is related to God, and therefore our knowledge of the Law is related to our knowledge of God Himself.

God and Self

But now—we must be getting on—likewise, a true knowledge of our own selfhood can only be had in connection with a true knowledge of God. Calvin brings out one aspect of this relationship at the opening of his famous *Institutio Religionis Christianae* (the "Institutes"). But actually, the correlativity of self-knowledge and God-knowledge is involved in the scriptural declaration that man was *created in the image of God*.[1]

All through the many centuries of western philosophic reflection men have repeatedly come back to this question of the Self, yet without much success. Man feels himself to be a radical, integral unity, but he cannot quite lay his hand on what that "sensed" unity is. The very popular contemporary British philosopher, Bertrand Russell, has summed up his reflection on the matter in this way: "Thus, in some sense it would seem we must be acquainted with our Selves as opposed to our particular experiences. But the question is difficult, and complicated arguments can be adduced on either side. Hence, although acquaintance with ourselves seems *probably* to occur, it is not wise to assert that it undoubtedly does occur."[2] Not a very rewarding result for all the thought and energy that have gone into the discussion!

Yet it is no wonder that men cannot fathom the deep mysteries of the Self. For they have treated the matter as though it were a philosophical question, or, more recently and particularly in America, a question of the so-called behavioural sciences (which latter it certainly can *not* be, as William Barrett has recently demonstrated[3]). It is, however, a *religious* question and can only be answered in the religious way. The Word of God, operat-

---

[1] By all means read Prof. Dooyeweerd's lecture "What is man?" in the volume Dooyeweerd, *In The Twilight of Western Thought*.

[2] B. Russell, *The Problems of Philosophy*, p. 51.

[3] William Barrett, *Irrational Man*, p. 260. This very recent book (1958) published by Doubleday all of you should certainly read. You will never be sorry.

ing as a POWER in our hearts, reveals God to us, but also our own selfhood in its radical, integral unity. Just as God is revealed as the Creator, the absolute and integral Origin of all things Who knows and can have no second Origin—e.g. Matter—over against or in addition to Himself (this in contrast with all the various types of dualism: the gnosticism of the first Christian centuries, the Manichaeans of the time of Augustine of Hippo, the Cathari of the medieval church, etc.), so man, created in His image, is revealed to himself in the religious root-unity of his creaturely existence (the 'heart'). However much diversity there may be in his life, that can never be construed as a diversity of two fundamentally different kinds, i.e. as the "being" of two "worlds" that have nothing whatsoever to do with each other (e.g. MATTER—What is that? *Never* mind!—and MIND—What is that? *No* matter), but must rather be "seen" as so many aspects of his central and integral religious being. Man is not a spirit that serves God and *also* a body belonging to the "world" of Galilean physics (and alien to the God-relation); man is servant of God in his entirety, *with nothing left over*. In singleness of heart man is to serve God. In him there is the same integrality that there is in the God Whom he images.

I am tempted here to expand, and also to go on and show how in the various thinkers there is a striking parallel between the view of God they develop and their view of the human self. But there is no time for it now. The point that has engaged us here, you will remember, is that our knowledge of God and our knowledge of our own selfhood are not two independent "knowledges"; they are *related*.

Law and Self

In the third place, there is a relation between our knowledge of Law and our knowledge of our own selves, and that, again, because Law and Self are related.

Luther, educated in the Occamist tradition, was inclined to put the freedom of the Christian man *over against* Law. To be in Christ is to be free, but to be free is to be *freed from the Law*, lifted up to the higher plane where Love reigns. There is in this life a voluntary submission to the laws of the state, for example, in accordance with the divine command, but essentially the man in Christ is freed from the Law. Gospel and Law exclude each other even where the Christian attempts to permeate the world of law with the love of the Gospel.

In the Bible, contrariwise, Law is not something of an inferior nature, not something to be freed from, but just the very condition of our existence as selves. One can think abstractly about freedom, and many do; in fact, it is the curse of the modern world. R. B. Kuiper, one-time chairman of the faculty of Westminster Theological Seminary and later president of Calvin Seminary, uses the illustration of the—slightly peculiar—old lady who went to visit a friend. When her hostess disappeared into her kitchen for a few minutes, this peculiar lady got up out of her chair and, walking about the salon, found a bowl of tropical fish behind the grand piano. In a sudden inspiration she reached her hand into the bowl, lifted out one of the fish and dropped it tenderly onto the rich carpeting that covered the floor. As she did so she muttered to herself, "Wicked old woman, keeping you shut up in that little old bowl! I'm going to give you the freedom of this whole salon." Of course, the fish promptly proceeded to *expire*. Why? Because it had been removed from that law-area for which it had been created. And so it is also with man: he can be free to live as man only when he is in the Law-environment for which he was created. That "environment" is the full range of the divine Law for the creation, is every law-word that proceeds from the mouth of God. In this sense the Law is the condition of man's freedom.[1]

The world-order is thus an order of law, a law-order; the Law holds everywhere. It holds also for man; indeed, man is embedded in it. Law is everywhere the *indispensable condition of life,* the all-encompassing context of our lives. Notice that in Romans 7:12, 14 Paul calls the Law holy, just, good and spiritual. If the creation is good, so is the Law.

It is only when we are not in a right relation to the Law that we feel Law as a curse, as something that blinds and limits us in a way that is undesirable, something that takes away our freedom. But then we must not condemn the Law, but convert ourselves. Read again Romans 7:14ff. And we must acquire a

---

[1] On this you must read the fundamental discussion of Dooyeweerd in his *New Critique of Theoretical Thought,* Vol. I, p. 511-523.

true view of freedom. When we sing the well-known hymn "Free from the law, O happy condition", we are not declaring ourselves free from the Law of God as the Law-structure of the creation. That would be Revolution, pure and simple. We must remember the second line of the hymn: "Jesus has bled, and there is remission". And perhaps even more pointed is the hymn that begins: "Make me a captive, Lord, and then I shall be free; force me to render up my sword, and I shall conqueror be".

In the course of modern philosophy there have been those who stressed Law so much (actually, absolutized it) that the Self disintegrated into a mere law-function. Take the great metaphysical systems of the seventeenth century, which looked to mathematics and physics for their model. On the other hand, the romantics who reacted against such a way of thinking so absolutized the Self (the Genius *is* the Law; when Mozart plays, that is the Law for musical production) that Law dissolved into the functioning of the human subject. Scripture, however, shows us the integral relation of Law and Self. Man is placed in the sphere of the Divine Law. When he does not maintain his right relation to the Law he becomes un-right-eous. Christ, the second Adam, keeps the whole Law (man must live by every word that proceedeth from the mouth of God) perfectly. His righteousness is declared to be that of God's people (justification), and is actually worked into their lives through the operations of the Holy Spirit (sanctification). Man becomes righteous again, and knows the Law as good. Without a true insight into the relation of Law and Self or Subject one cannot understand the Christian religion.

Sometimes one runs across something of an insight into the real relation of Self and Law in quite unexpected places. In his book *Modern French Literature* Denis Saurat writes (p. 79) as follows about the difference between nineteenth and twentieth century French literature: "The conception of a moral law has disappeared. Mallarmé and Baudelaire rebelled against the moral law because there was one . . . For Gide, Proust, Valery, Malraux, Montherlant there is no law. There is no thrill in breaking the law . . . *Le moi* (the Self) also has disappeared. *Le Culte du moi* of Barres' early work no longer means anything. There is no *moi*. Proust's Marcel does not know what his *moi* is—and does not care. Perhaps *le moi* was connected with the law, formed itself, as in Corneille, in submitting to the law, or, as in Baudelaire, in rebelling against it. But now, no law and no *moi*." We can only add: just so!

One Insight

I think we have now discussed the relations of God and Law and Self sufficiently for our present purposes, and we have seen that our knowledge of these three is not a matter of three separate "knowledges". These "knowledges" are *related*. In the light of our discussion, however, I think we can now go a step farther and say that *a true knowledge of the three comes as one insight*. It is not that we make analytical corrections in one 'item' and then go on to adjust the other two, or any such thing. This knowledge is a knowledge of the "heart", the religious concentration point of our existence; it comes in a single flash of insight; it brings us world-orientation and thus sets our lives going in the right direction. (Cf. Ps. 86:11 and Ps. 25:12-14)

Permit me a rather simple illustration of what I mean. Let us suppose that Christ Himself should suddenly appear visibly in His glory right here in this room. You know what would happen. Each one of us would be down on his knees. We would be vividly aware of three things: (1) that this Person is the Sovereign Lord; (2) that we are nothing in ourselves over against Him, but solely and wholly His servants; (3) that His Word is our Law. In effect we would be saying, "Speak, Lord; for thy servant heareth", and in that response of our hearts the three "knowledges" of which we have been speaking are found: (1) Lord (God); (2) thy servant (self); (3) speak . . . heareth (the Law-word). Such knowledge is not analytical knowledge, with its multiplicity of items and processes; it is *a single insight,* present in the religious depth-level of our existence previous to all analysis. It comes when we are confronted with the Word of God.

The Word of God is the POWER by which God opens our hearts to see our human situation in the framework of the whole of reality. This is to know the Truth. And to know the Truth is wisdom; for the fear of Jehovah, you will remember, is the starting-point of wisdom. Possessed of wisdom, we know how to live out our lives. We have the *regula* or principle by which to direct our goings.

But the Word of God does more. We are not only made aware of our place in the creation, but we are also convicted of our sin. In the presence of Christ we know not merely that we are nothing but servants; we know also that we are *unworthy* servants, not in part, but wholly. And, further, we know the total redemption of Christ. In a flash we know our place, that we have (in the first Adam) fallen from our place, and that in the second Adam we are restored to our place (though only in Him). It is not true that only part of us is fallen (e.g. the bodily passions), because there are no "parts". The *integrality* of the creation (particularly in the heart of man) brings with it the *radical* character of the Fall. In the Fall of man all created reality was directed away from the service of God. But it is also true that in the saving work of Christ in the heart of man all the creation is re-directed to the service and glorification of God.

I hope that the foregoing discussions will have served to elucidate what we mean when we say that the Word of God is the POWER that works in us an existential awareness of the integral creation-order and (within that Order) of the radical Fall and the radical Restoration in Christ. Now, perhaps, we can begin to understand how the Word of God is centrally relevant for all our learning. For in our learning we are everywhere confronted not only with a great diversity of states of affairs, but with an Order of states of affairs. Facts do not "speak" to us unless we see them in their Order. In one way or another the scholar must have an Order in his findings. If the Word of God does not teach him what this Order is, he must substitute some principle of total-structuration of his own devising. Now in opposition to all such principles of human devising (about which we shall speak in the next lecture) the Word of God posits the Truth. It is the *Divine Thesis*, of which all human substitutes can be only so many Distortions.

Lecture II

Antithesis

Yesterday is was Thesis; today it is Antithesis. Before I finish today I shall have to clarify the sense of the word antithesis as I am using it here. First, however, a quick review of how far we have come is, I think, in order. Recapitulation, one of the men present here yesterday reminded us, is important. I should like therefore to recapitulate very briefly what I tried to say in the first lecture, but in the process I may just add to what I said then. This is to say that my purpose is not merely to recapitulate, but rather by means of the recapitulation to get us all back on the track of thought of these lectures.

The Word and the World of Learning

You will recall that I began yesterday by describing two fundamentally diverging ways the Dutch Calvinist immigration in Canada can take, and that I then proposed that the way you ultimately will go will be determined by whether or not you have seen clearly the *inner connection that exists* between the Word of God and our life in this world, more particularly just now the *intrinsic connection between that Word and the world of learning*. The first thing that had to occupy our attention therefore was the question, just what, precisely, is the Word of God? To see that clearly is the first requirement for really seeing the need of Christian action in our society and of a Christian centre of higher studies and research on this North American continent.

I have a little hope that already many of you are beginning

to be able to picture to yourselves, at least in some tentative way, how the land appears to us to lie. But today's lecture ought to help greatly in fixing that picture in your minds.

We saw that the Word of God in all its many words is yet one Word in that as a POWER operating upon our hearts it reveals to us, in the twinkling of an eye, God Himself, our own self, and the world-order, the cosmos of God's creation-ordinances in which we have been placed to serve God before His face in single-hearted covenantal obedience and love. It is as though the Word (Voice) of God addresses us: "Adam," "Samuel," YOU (fill in your own name), and at once we know the whole Truth. With Samuel we say, "Speak, Lord; for thy servant heareth." That is, Thou art the LORD; Thy word is the law; I am nothing but Thy servant. I am, further, an unworthy servant, but Thou hast called me back to service. Thus the Word of God reveals at once our total human situation, not merely the situation as given in the order of creation, but also, within that situation, our Fall from our Place in the cosmos as imaging vice-gerent—"Adam, where art thou?"—and our complete and glorious Restoration to it in Jesus Christ, the second and substitutionary Adam.

The Word of God is thus God's Word of Truth about the ultimate nature of things: who we men are (our "heredity"); in what kind of location we have been put by God (our "environment"); what, in the light of the previous two, we have to do (i.e. how to walk in the Truth). As such a POWER the Word of God is God's THESIS, the first and only True Statement, by which the nature of our life in the world is elucidated and its way (thus) directed.

Here then we found that oneness of the Word of God. In our thinking and speaking about that Word we men are required to think successively a number of thoughts and use a multiplicity of words. We can never quite reach the unity, cannot put our fingers solidly on it, as is also the case with our thinking about our own selfhood. The unity is just beyond our logical grasp; yet *religiously* we are aware that the unity is there. By means of this converting Word, this Word that begets us to new life, the sovereign, the living God takes hold of us in the religious heart or concentration-point of our existence and *sets us in the Truth,* i.e. in Christ.

The Meaning of Truth

I must add right here that all this is of fundamental importance for our understanding the meaning of the word "truth." We had some debate about that word yesterday, you will remember. It comes up repeatedly in my classes at Calvin too. I am constantly being asked, Isn't 2 plus 2 equals 4 a "truth"? Isn't the fact that the combining of one chemical element with another produces uniformly a certain kind of chemical combination a "truth"? To all such questions I reply that we must distinguish between a more or less correct description of those limited states of affairs that immediately press upon us all and the truth about those states of affairs. The *truth* of them cannot be seen in isolation from the whole coherence of meaning of the creation-order as seen in the light of God's Word. It is important to remember in this connection that we must always be "normed" by Scripture, and Scripture tells us what the Truth is. The Word of God is God's Word of Truth. (Jas. 1:18). Christ is the Word of God, and the Truth. Scripture commands us to stand in the Truth, to stand in Jesus Christ. And that is, of course, our norm. When we talk about the Truth we must remember that Truth in the Scripture is not some discrete (cut off, separate, abstracted from the totality) observation of positively given phenomena, such a notion of "truth" as nineteenth century positivism defended and handed on to phenomenology. Truth in the Scripture has to do with the whole of reality in its central religious meaning. Only the Word of God, by which we are ingrafted into Christ can set us in the Truth!

Removing Possible Misunderstandings

This is probably the place, before we go on to new material, to attempt to remove a couple of possible misunderstandings with respect to the development of our thought thus far. First, then, one of the ministers who was present yesterday asked, after my lecture, whether I had given proper emphasis to the Church, and especially to the fact that we come to the Word of God through the Church. Now, of course, the Church and its proclamation of the Word of God is of primary importance in the dynamic development of the Kingdom of God, and it is certainly true that it is through the presence of the Church in the world that we come to hear the Word of God. But in these lectures I am concerned with the *transcendence* of the Word of God. It is the Word that is first. The confessing Church is one manifestation of the Body of Christ, but the Body of Christ (Kingdom of God) is just that Body of believers, that Fellowship, that Community of faith that the Spirit gathers by the *Word*. We must never forget that God's work in the heart is first; God *establishes* His Church by His Word. That is why it was not necessary for me in the present context to speak particularly of the Church.

A second misunderstanding that might possibly have arisen in your minds concerns my statement that the central thrust of the Word of God is the revelation of: 1) an (integral) Creation; 2) the (radical) Fall; and 3) the (equally radical) Restoration in Jesus Christ. In the Netherlands Prof. Dr. C. A. van Peursen in his book *Filosofische Oriëntatie* (Kok, Kampen, 1958), p. 132, has raised the objection to this procedure that any such statement as to the central thrust of the Bible is itself the result of our own human, thus fallible, exegesis or effort at interpretation, subject therefore to all the relativity of historical and theological influences out of the past, and that other persons, from a different perspective, can just as well suggest some other formulation. He mentions, for one, the Kingdom of God as a possibility.

To this I should like to answer, first, that I cannot see how Van Peursen's suggestion that someone might put over against our formulation that of the Kingdom of God can do anything but establish and confirm what we have said here. For if we stop for one minute to reflect on the idea of the Kingdom of God we find that it is the Kingdom of men redeemed in Christ. And that means that God in Christ has caused man, who fell in the whole of his being from his representative place or office, to stand once again, that is, to stand righteous (in Christ, of course) in the entire Law-order of God. Thus the Kingdom itself requires for its understanding the central theme of integral Creation, radical Fall and radical Restoration. That *is* the Kingdom, the Kingdom of the re-new-ed Righteousness of God.

But, second, and more basic, we must, I repeat, get away from the notion that the Bible is simply a communication to this "world" (?) objectively (i.e. not impinging on me, the subject) of a body of judgments to which I, man, come with my apparatus for rational understanding. By His Word God begets us to a new life. By His Word He *attaches* us to the Truth. Suddenly we "see" the nature of the real. We "see" the universe at its heart to be that great covenantal commerce between God and His image and vice-gerent, man, who, in the whole of that Sure Order of Law that is the creation, is to walk in holiness before his God, making all his cultural work in the creation (established by the cultural Mandate) to correspond with the demands of the divine law-ordinances and thus to be his religious service to God. (Study Rom. 12:1 in the light of its context, i.e. preceded by ch. 11 and followed by ch. 13.) We "see" ourselves as integral (i.e. that there is no *remnant* that is *not* concentrated in this covenantal relation) in an integral creation-order (i.e. no second principle such as Matter over against, alien to, not concentrated upon God through man in his integral heart-service). From the standpoint of Scripture there can be no Being (matter or substance) that is not related to, concentrated upon this covenantal centre of reality. There can be no "qualities" in themselves, that are not seen as related to man's cultural-religious service in the Covenant. There can be no "image" of God in man apart from his total representative place. It is extremely important that we leave off all the old orthodox-scholastic notions of the image of God as being related to some substance some rational substance in me, some *structural* thing that is to be found in all men. I should like to suggest a book for you to read on this subject, one of the volumes of Prof. Berkouwer's Dogmatische Studiën, viz. *De Mens het Beeld Gods*, Kok, Kampen, 1957. It has been translated into English under the title: *Man, the Image of God*.

The Ordering Principle of Life

It is, I think, becoming clearer as we go on with the lectures that the Word of God is indeed the ordering principle of our life, the principle that gives order to all our experience. We said yesterday, you will remember, that our question about the relation of the Word of God to our life in this world, including our life in the "world" of learning, is the question about *principles*. I said that we may sometimes have talked too abstractly about our principles. Our esteemed colleague here in this conference, Prof. Van Riessen, has said the same thing in his book *De Maatschappij der Toekomst*—English translation, *The Society of the Future*—and he has said it very well. It is one of the best statements about it I have ever read anywhere. Be sure to read especially his third and seventh chapters, entitled "Structural Principles of Society" and "The Liberation of Society" respectively. It is better to read the Dutch text, if you can, than the English (which sometimes misses the point even on central issues). 'Principle' is the Origin that orders, structurates. The Word of God, understood as the POWER of God that opens our hearts to the Truth, is thus the principle of our life.

Many so-called detailed problems will suddenly be illuminated when seen in connection with the central principle. Take, for instance, the problem of responsibility, closely related to the matter of man's imaging God. Older thinkers, heavily influenced by alien (to Christianity) rationalistic ways of thinking, who accordingly took the image to be what they called Reason, thus supposedly identifying the image with something in the *structure* of man considered separate from the *directedness* of his life to God, frequently thought of man's responsibility as following from his rationality. This is still today repeatedly being said by many Calvinist professors and thinkers. Man is rational, they argue. That is to say, he can distinguish by means of concepts differences in things. For that reason he can also distinguish between right and wrong. And therefore he is responsible. Constantly you will run across some such line of thought. But it is not true, as you can see as soon you relate the question of responsibility to our central principle, the Word of God. From Scripture it should be clear that our human responsibility arises not from the fact that we have within us something called rationality, but just exactly from the central religious place we have in the Cosmos, God's representative in the Creation, put over against His face in the Covenant, made subject to His Law, given our human task to carry out in religious loving obedience. Of course it is true that the rational or analytical aspect of our life is always *present in* our responsibility, but many other aspects of our temporal life are also involved. Responsibility however is a matter not of one of these aspects but of the total situation in its religious concentration of meaning.

So much then to point up the power of the ordering principle to "place" and thus elucidate much that is often taken to be detailed questions. It is, indeed, in the light of our principle that we see the connection of all the details of our life. Christ, Kingdom of God, Righteousness, State, marriage, family, Covenant, Church, —how they all come together into a beautiful unity. I am sorry that we cannot here take the time to talk about it. At this point the Groen Club booklet *The Bible and the Life of the Christian,* will, I think, be of great help to you. It deals specifically with these topics.

God, Self and Cosmos. *The Metaphysical Questions par excellence*

We must, however, be getting on to the material that belongs more particularly to our subject matter for today. And, now, the first thing that has to be pointed out is this, that from the beginning of western philosophical speculation that speculation has centered about the three moments of God, Self and the World-order, order of nature, Nature, or whatever you may for the moment wish to call it. I think it was Prof. Cornford in his book *From Religion to Philosophy* who remarked about Thales— many have looked upon Thales (I think, incorrectly; cf. Werner Jaeger, *The Theology of the Early Greek Philosophers*, ch. 1) as the first of the Greek philosophers—that when he said that everything is full of gods and souls and that everything is water he was operating with the three core-conceptions of previous Greek religion: God, the Self, the World-order (the world all reduces to one stuff, water). These questions that philosophy inherits were religious questions, and, as we have seen, only in the religious way can the truth about them be known. Yet these very problems became the heart of philosophical speculation, of what we know as metaphysics.

The history of metaphysical speculation can thus never be understood unless we see it as a new way of attempting to find answers to questions that really are religious. They are religious questions because we cannot properly formulate them or answer them except by being in a covenantal fellowship of life with God, except by being taken hold of in our hearts and set in the Truth. They *became* metaphysical questions when they were taken to be questions that can be answered by a supposed purely rational analysis of our temporal existence, considered as independent of the religious relation.

This *metaphysical* attempt to find answers to these questions lasted right down through the centuries until we arrive at Immanuel Kant's *Critique of Pure Reason*. In the section of that *Critique* called the Transcendental Dialectic, Book II we find a discussion of the three questions of 1) a rational or speculative anthropology or psychology (the Paralogisms), the question of the "I" or Self; 2) a rational or speculative cosmology (the Antinomies), the question of the world-order; and 3) a rational or speculative theology, the theistic proofs for the existence of God. Here we have the very heart of that Dialectic that became so important for the later idealistic developments through Hegel. Kant wished to destroy metaphysics *in this sense,* that any *theoretical* answers (theoretical in the sense of the scientific method of concept building) to these questions are impossible. He proposed however a *practical* reason which was supposed to be able to help here. He had to do away with *knowledge* here, he himself wrote, in order to make a place for *faith.* But faith was for Kant a kind of moralistic reflection, not Christian faith. Many followers of Kant drew a different lesson from his writing; they followed the agnostic-phenomenalistic way: metaphysics is impossible, and since our three questions were by all men taken to be metaphysical questions, no answer to these questions could be expected.

There was something good in this agnostic reaction to Kant. These questions can never be solved in the metaphysical way. But this dead-end result did not drive men to see the Light of the Word of God. The positivistic spirit took possession of the hearts of many men in the later nineteenth century in Europe, and has since become a mighty force in the academic centres of the Anglo-Saxon world in the twentieth.

More recent decades are showing however that there was something about the metaphysical movement that cannot be denied man. Our life is a life lived in an Order, and awareness of the Order is necessary in order to possess a significant knowledge even of "facts." "Facts" unordered do not "speak" to us. Even when the true sense of the Order is not clear, the Order itself is there, and that as revelation impinging upon us, and it asserts itself and appears in a man's imaginings in some distorted form. For we men cannot escape our creation-situation as men; we *are* not analytical fact-recording machines; we are God's representatives in the earth, before God's face to know (in the Hebrew sense) and live in the Truth. We are that prophet-priest-king creature, fallen from our office in Adam or restored to it in Christ. This unavoidable creation-situation drives men to give an answer to the religious core-questions. Kant wanted to prove that metaphysics is impossible. Well, so it is. But the central questions of metaphysics we found to be in actuality religious questions (known aright only when we are in the firm grip of the Word of God), and as such they remain at the centre of our human experience and insist on our prophetic-priestly-kingly response.

Understood in the above sense, metaphysics is always a human *substitution for living a truly religious life*. This is not to say, however, that there is no properly philosophical task. What it does mean is that there is no *autonomous* philosophical task, that is, one that is not directed from out of a deeper-lying religious level of our being.

The Nature of Sin and Grace

The present step in advancing our argument is most important to notice. The Fall does not change our creation-situation. The cosmos of God's Will (Law) remains firm. Man remains bound to God in a covenantal relationship, and is guilty therein. That is the meaning of his life. The Fall is simply a change in the *direction* we give to our lives. God remains the Sovereign, but we no longer acknowledge Him as such. The Law abides sure, the holy and gracious Law-word of our Creator-Lord for our life; we no longer bow under it as such. We men too continue to be nothing in ourselves; but we repress this and, cutting ourselves off in our imagining from the religious relation that is our true situation, we try to make ourselves to be something having its Ground in itself. A *substance,* for instance. Something that is just here, a Da-sein. The creation-meaning abides as faithful as the Word of God that called it into being and sustains it. We have to do something with *it;* it is all there is to do something with; there is no other reality than God's creation to be accounted for.

But having in our unrighteousness suppressed the Truth, we must imagine to ourselves (in our hearts) a Lie. An account of our total situation is inevitable because of our own nature. Thus we devise (imagine, conjure up) some new principle of the total-structuration of our life-experience. That is the Lie which is not according to reality but is a figment of our imagination. The positive affirmation (God's Word, the Truth) is first, the THESIS. Our Lie is the placing of a *repressing* and *supplanting* statement over against God's True Statement. The False Statement of ours is thus the Anti-thesis or ANTITHESIS. As Paul tells us in the first chapter of Romans, we men "exchanged the truth of God for a lie, and worshipped and served the creature rather than the Creator, who is blessed forever" (vs. 25). The result he describes in the next two verses (26, 27): our life-activities came to be directed against nature, i.e. against the cosmos of God's Law-word.

The Restoration work of Christ is thus not an addition of Grace to a Nature that is just here (and in a natural or normal condition). God's entire integral creation centers in Man. When we men fell the whole creation was turned by the heart of man away from its proper end or direction, viz. to glorify and serve the Creator. The Kingdom of Grace is the announcement that a new Head of the race has graciously been provided in the Second and Last Man. The Kingdom of God is the renewing of the heart. It is the new Righteousness. We men can stand once again in the Truth and "see" reality as it is. Consequently, we are brought back to an obedient bowing under the creation-ordinances.

In other words, grace does not *complete* nature (where nature is taken as a normal something not affected by Fall or Redemption internally), as Thomas Aquinas said and Roman Catholics believe. (We shall try to say more about this in our third lecture tomorrow). Rather, grace *renews nature.* In the Kingdom of Grace the creation norms are activated once again in the many relationships of life: parents and children, husband and wife, masters and servants, government and subjects. Right into the very heart of the Kingdom of Grace (the Church-institute) Christ maintains the creation-order.

Christ and the Creation-ordinances

It is important to emphasize this point today when from Barthian and other crisis-theology circles we are told that we must proceed only from Christ, and that there can be no mention of creation ordinances. Let me bring forward at this moment only two examples of what I mean. First, the question of divorce. In Matthew 19 we read what Christ said to the Pharisees who asked him about it to test him. Christ refers them to the creation: "Have ye not read that he who made them from the beginning made them male and female, and said, For this cause shall a man leave his father and mother, and shall cleave to his wife; and the two shall become one flesh?" The Pharisees strike back, you remember, and remind our Lord that Moses commanded to give a bill of divorcement. To this Christ made reply, "Moses for your hardness of heart suffered you to put away your wives; but from the *beginning* it hath not been so." That is, the government (Moses) must take the condition of the people into consideration in the forming of its legislation; it must work "christelijk-historisch," as the Christian statesmen of the Netherlands have always said. But the proclamation of the Truth in Christ points back to the Law-demands of the creation-order.

A second example is what Paul says about women's wearing hats in the churches. His word is often relativized as simply a reference to the *mores* or customs of his day. But significantly that is not what Paul is doing. He grounds his argument in the creation-situation. According to the original ordinance of the Father the woman does not stand on a par with the man. Read I Cor. 11:5-10, and compare I Tim. 2:9-15. For *that* reason the woman should not enter the congregation with uncovered head. Here again we have in the proclamation of Christ's Kingdom an appeal to the original creation-ordinance. It is for such reasons that the Kingdom can also be called Righteousness. For it is through the reign of Christ *according to the Law of God* that man is again restored to the proper relation to God and his fellow-men. Christ maintained the proper relation as Second Man: He stood righteous. His righteousness is accounted *and made* our righteousness in the Kingdom of Righteousness.

Antithesis as Systematic (religious) Distortion of Creation-Order

But we must be getting back to the main point we were making. Even in the Fall we remain *religious* beings, possessed of some vaguely haunting awareness of our integral selfhood and of a cosmic law, as well as of God. Take the Self, for example. We have a sense that somehow all our life-activities come together into one, a oneness that is the "I", the *moi*, the Self. We simply cannot *locate* or identify any longer that root-unity of our lives to our own satisfaction and so that we and others are convinced. The meaning of the "I" escapes us. Yet we are somehow driven to keep on trying to fix it in a statement about what that deeper unity is. (In other words, fallen man, just because he remains the religiously-bound creature God made him, does not simply act as a rational analyzer of "facts" that are positively presented to his senses or mind. As a religious being he is driven to religious statements, to a search for the totality of meaning and to make a statement about the unity of his selfhood.

We have already seen, however, that true self-knowledge arises only in a living fellowship with God. And it is that fellowship that fallen man has broken. He is now no longer in a position to see the great diversity of aspects of his temporal life *as concentrated in the religious heart and directed to the Origin of his life*. He worships the creature, removed in imagination from any relation to the Creator. He thinks of himself as just this thing here. But since this something that is just here, our temporal existence, exhibits a great diversity of moments or aspects—e.g. numerical, spatial, physical (kinematic), energetic, organic, psychical, analytical, historial-technical, lingual, social, economic, aesthetic, jural, ethical and pistical—, and all of them, seen in the Light of the Word of God are *relative aspects, components,* of the religious root-unity (our life as a whole is religion) that is concentrated upon the worship of God, apostate man is driven by his religious needs to find a substitute to fill in for the true root-unity of his life he is religiously eluding, to *absolutize* one of the relative aspects or sides of our religious life and *elevate* it to the place of the heart. In doing this he is not, as you can see, merely picking up sense-images of reality on the blank tablet of his mind. He must find an absolute in the relative. We see him *bound to the creation-structure:* he must know himself. At the same time we see him *wilfully substituting his Lie to replace the Truth. He must have his absolute, even if it means that he must distort what observation will readily disclose to be relative. His rational analysis is accompanied by the deeper drive, which in the fallen state requires a distortion of the very "facts" he is in the process of analyzing.*

An immediately apparent example of what I am talking about is offered by the contemporary irrationalist attack upon the old rationalist theory of man as Reason. "Reason" is actually an apostate concept; it is a myth. It arises from an absolutization and deification of our analytical capacity to distinguish difference conceptually. The apostate need for a "substantial" entity that is just there has taken hold of a relative function of our temporal existence (relative, because an analysis of our analytical-functional life discloses a multiplicity of moments in it that requires the other life-moments of our temporal existence in order to be) and distorted it into being a something, the central "thing" of our life. Rationalism assumed that the heart of man was Reason.

Yet this rationalistic account is actually wholly at variance with observable states of affairs. Recent researches in psychology, psychoanalysis and of various social philosophers would seem to render highly dubious the existence of any such Reason as rationalism had assumed. We can note the change that has taken place by observing the changed meaning of the verb "to rationalize." In earlier centuries "to rationalize" one's conduct meant to bring forward the rational or logical grounds for it. Today "to rationalize" would more likely mean, at least in many quarters, "to make to look rational what was done for 'reasons' that are really subrational, 'reasons' that lie in the dark folds and murky depths of the psychical life." In other words, "rationalize" now refers more to a mask on the surface than to the central heart of man. In irrationalism Reason has been removed from its supposed central position and made peripheral and relative. Of course, we may add that irrationalism in turn has taken some other relative aspect of our temporal existence that is no more central than the old "Reason" of the rationalists, and made *it* the "heart."

Great Diversity of Antitheses

Our illustration brings us to the next point, viz. that apostate men do not always agree on what they absolutize. This ought not to surprise us at all. Oneness of mind (or heart: concord), unity, community, peace,—these are the fruit of God's uniting our hearts in a fellowship of faith by the POWER of His Word. Where men are not so bound, nothing is there to prevent their seizing first upon one and then upon another of the many aspects of our temporal life as being in their view the absolute origin of the other aspects. This is made possible by the very relative character of each of the life-aspects: being relative, the other meaning-aspects of life are involved in their very nature. The wholeness of meaning is present universally in a certain way in each aspect. It requires but a distortion of this creation-structure to see one aspect as the *fulness* of meaning required for the heart of all the other meaning-aspects. I shall return to this yet obscure point next time.

So it is that a great diversity of Antitheses has arisen in the course of philosophical history. We have spoken of rationalism; but we know also an aestheticism, a materialism, an organicism, a technicism, and so on. Man has been conceived of as a rational being, as a material organization, as a technical being, as an economic being. You have probably heard the terms: man the machine, *homo faber, homo oeconomicus,* etc. These, and others I shall not take the time to mention, are all totality-views about man that arise not from a mere rational observation and analysis of positive facts presented to our "minds"—if that were so, conflict between them would be lacking—, but rather from a failure to see the relative aspects of our life as all relative, and from the consequent effort to explain all the remaining relative aspects in terms of one that is (religiously) lifted out or absolutized, and thus made the deeper source and unity of the others.

You will notice that for the several "theories" that thus arose we use these "ism" words. These words always indicate distortion, exaggeration. We "feel" the distortion and speak of the theory as being one-sided. When this onesidedness has been sufficiently felt a change may come to another theory. But in time it too proves to be one-sided. There never comes a resting-point, a satisfactory end to the search. Man does not find himself. So much is this the case that many modern men have made a virtue of the evil and said they would rather have an eternal search for the truth than have the truth in their possession. The latter, they pretend to themselves, is fit for the gods alone.

In these three lectures it is impossible to go into all these highly complicated matters. All I can hope to do is to be suggestive, to provide a certain stimulus for you to go and work more efficiently with the books that are available. Rush to the book table at the back of the room after the lectures. The lectures ought to set you to reading important books. I can only hope to give you an initial momentum, as it were, to set you to the task for yourselves. Only then do you become a student.

The important thing in this Conference is that you begin to see how the Word of God really *directs* us in our analysis of our experience. What the Word of God does not do, of course, is to tell us that there are fourteen or so aspects, law-spheres, ways (modes, modalities) in which that which is, is. For that is strictly a matter of analysis. The Word directs us however to take whatever diversity of moments we find in the creation as *a diversity of the integral fulness of meaning of our religious life.* In this way the Word directs us to the integral creation-order concentrated in the heart of man, and at the same time liberates us from

~~old Greek ways of interpret~~ing our experience ~~that in one~~ modi-
~~fication or another have pretty largely~~ kept their hold on us down
to the present.

The Failure of Greek Thought

For the Greeks never "saw" the integral structure of the creation. How could they? Separated from the Sovereign God they missed any true knowledge of their own selfhood. They were lost in the functional diversity of this temporal life and had no awareness further of the religious depth-level of human existence; whatever they might think of themselves would have to be in terms of the temporal diversity.

A notable peculiarity of the Greek outlook is the way man and the world-order are seen as a conjoining or bundling together of a higher and a lower "world." This peculiarity seems to have arisen out of the religious-historical experience of the peoples in the Greek area. There seems to have been an earlier stratum of tradition that was characterized by a *natural* cult-religion (finding gods or divine powers in a sudden waterfall, a peculiar flight of birds, the explosive power of the acorn or some similar organic or physical phenomenon) with its correspondingly *naturalistic-religious* way of explaining man's life and the world in which he lives. A later movement then appears to have entered the scene with the Olympian deities, which are personalized *cultural* powers of man, and this tradition thinks of man, instead of in terms of his physical-organic life, more as a cultural being (engaged in thought and technics, concerned with the beautiful and the good). These two traditions apparently slowly intermingled, the cultural conception being superimposed upon but only partially conquering the naturalistic conception. In man therefore "body" and "soul" stand for these two previous ways of conceiving man as a totality (each thus an apostate distortion of the integral nature of man), but in classical Greek thought the two are brought together into an amalgam. Further, the "soul-concept" of the later cultural movement is thought of as closer to the nature of the (conquering Olympian) deities, as "superior," of a higher ontic status, while the "body-concept" is thought of as "inferior."

Thus we get the peculiar Greek division of everything into a higher "world" and a lower "world." Remember that each of these "worlds" was originally an apostate distortion of the integral creation-order, arising from a lack of insight into the central religious meaning of the creation and resulting in the absolutization of a natural "aspect" or a cultural "aspect" of that creation-meaning. When the two have been brought together, and each relativized with respect to the other, we are no closer to an insight into the root-unity of man's life or the integral meaning of the Cosmos of God.

In the Word of God "body" cannot mean some lower or inferior "part" of me, opposed to the more god-like "soul." Such a conception is simply foreign to the Bible. Take, for instance, Romans 12:1. We are to present our *bodies* a living sacrifice unto God. Surely that cannot mean that I am to present my inferior, more animal-like nature as a sacrifice of life unto God! No; in the Bible we hear of the whole man *outwardly* (the body) and the whole *inner* man-in-religious-concentration-upon-his-Origin (the soul or heart). Paul speaks of the outward and inward man (II Cor. 4:16). But each of these is the whole man. Such a view is governed by the basic religious motive of the Word of God: the *integral* creation, the *radical* (because piercing to the integral root) Fall and Redemption, and is in antithetical relation to any Greek view of body and soul as a lower and higher "world."

The Influence of Apostate Principles

Yet the Greek views of dichotomy and trichotomy—some Greek philosophers added a "pneuma", Latin, *spiritus,* above the *soma* (body) and *psyche* (soul)—entered the Christian Church through the early Church Fathers, and represented such a powerful tradition of thought that few have ever escaped their clutches. Many Christians to this day, accepting a more or less Greek view of body-substance and soul-substance, are forever engaged with the problems associated with the names of traducianism and creationism. I do not know whether you are all aware of what these matters mean. Perhaps somewhere you have heard a discussion about whether and when God creates a soul and slips it into the procreated bodily substance, or whether the "soul-stuff" is passed along somehow with the "physical stuff."

The Word of God shows up all these problems as *pseudo*-problems. They are not genuine problems. Yet think of the centuries of theological reflection that have been directed away from the central issues of the Word-revelation to these pseudo-problems! And of the devastating effect that the prominence given to such Hellenized theology has had upon the Church's witness and catechizing and preaching! And think of all the Christians through all the centuries who have come back in the western centres of academic work, come back time after time in their philosophical endeavours, in psychology, anthropology, and other sciences to attempt still another solution for these pseudo-problems. Of course, their effort was always in vain, because the distorted formulation at the outset precluded their analytically probing the *really* existing states of affairs in the world. If you know anything of the history of these sciences you know too well the unhappy situation that I am speaking about. How long we have allowed ourselves to be slaves to idols! But oh, the liberating POWER of the Word of God!

All the special sciences have been fundamentally affected by the mighty tradition of setting up a "world" of Matter (e.g. the so-called "world" of Galilean physics) over against another "world" of Mind; a "world" of brute "facts" over against a "world" of human "values"; a "world" of the objective (the "external" world of the content of consciousness) over against an "inner world" of the subjective (the human consciousness). Does mathematics belong to the world of Mind or to the world of material things? If to both, what possible relation can exist between these two "worlds"? Are the laws for logical reasoning laws in the world of Mind, norm-laws? Then have they nothing to do with the world of natural facts that is analyzed? What is the relation of norm-laws to natural laws? Is man a rational ghost in a machine? If man is soul and body (in the sense of higher and lower parts), then how explain the somehow still sensed *unity* of Self? You have undoubtedly heard of the whole series of tortured theoretical attempt to force a unity after having started with a twoness, attempts that go by such established names as interactionism, parallelism, occasionalism, ennoetism, impetus theory, hylemorphism, etc. In linguistic science, as in all the other sciences, you get a great variety of schools of interpretation of the phenomenon of language: materialistist, organicist, psychologistic, technicistic, etc.

Apostate principles of total-structuration have had an influence nothing short of calamitous upon social development and our social studies. Not having any insight into the central Kingdom-rule of Christ, men have failed to observe the *limitations* of delegated authorities granted to human office-bearers in church, state, family, marriage, etc. The totalitarian idea of the cult and of the state are found everywhere. Always an aspect of the temporal diversity of our life has been lifted out, absolutized to take the place of the repressed central, total Rule of Christ. Think of the so-called Christian Middle Ages with their long struggle between the two totalitarian powers of Emperor and Pope![1]

There is no time to go into all these matters now. But I do want you to begin to see how the great principles of total-structuration of our experience work themselves out in the fundamental problems of all the special sciences. As we have seen, the positivists of the 19th and 20th centuries tried to make the special sciences autonomous wih respect to philosophy, and looked upon philosophy as something quite indifferent from the standpoint of their own supposedly empirical research of limited states of affairs. Perhaps I can dispense most quickly with this matter by offering you a short quotation from Prof. H. Dooyeweerd's *A New Critique of Theoretical Thought* (Vol. I, p. 548): "It is impossible to establish a line of demarcation between philosophy and science in order to *emancipate the latter from the former*. Science cannot be isolated in such a way as to give it a completely independent sphere of investigation and any attempt to do so cannot withstand a serious critique. It would make sense to speak of the autonomy of the special sciences if, and only if, a special science could actually investigate a specific aspect of temporal reality without theoretically considering its coherence with the other aspects. No scientific thought, however, is possible in such isolation 'with closed shutters'. Scientific thought is constantly confronted with the temporal coherence of meaning among the modal aspects of reality, and cannot escape from following a transcendental Idea of this coherence . . . even the special sciences investigating the first two modal aspects of human experience, i.e. the arithmetical and the spatial, cannot avoid making philosophical presuppositions in this sense." (Read the whole section there, Vol. I, pp. 545-556.)

Fundamentally, that is the reason that we must have an

---

[1] See *Christian Perspectives*, 1961, pp. 80-84.

integral development of both philosophy and all the special sciences out of their common religious starting-point in the Word-revelation of the Truth. Nothing short of a centre of higher studies where all the work arises from a radically scriptural point of departure, a fellowship in the Truth, can be of any real help to us in the very critical and very complicated needs of our twentieth century society. The philosopher needs the special scientist, and vice versa. But neither can satisfy the other's needs except they both experience an organic growth of mind in a common submission to the Word of God. *That* is what makes a Christian university or a Christian centre of research and higher studies. Not a group of persons alone; but a common Principle. For persons are always directed by such a Principle.

Distortions of the Law

Before I conclude this already heavy lecture, I must call your attention to one more type of apostate distortion. I refer to distortions with respect to the Law. In dealing with the Law we are dealing with the most basic problem of philosophy. For this whole universe is a Law-order, subject to the Creator's holy will. Everything within and without us is lawful, full of law, law-states. The Law of God is the all-encompassing environment of our lives that both marks off the creation from the Creator and also ties it to Him. To know God is to know the Law as His *Will for* what He calls into being. The Law is other than the creation, as it is other than God Himself. God *creates* the cosmos; He *puts* His Law. The creation *is;* the Law *holds* or *obtains*.

The Greeks, who had no true knowledge of the sovereign Lawgiver, could not have a true knowledge of the Law either. They easily forgot that the Law comes from *without* the cosmos, is *put* by God *to* the cosmos. So it was that views arose first which *identified the Law with some portion of the cosmos*. Since, as we have seen, the Greeks no longer "saw" the central religious depth-level of cosmic existence, the Law came naturally to be identified with (a part of) the *functional* cosmos, with some kind of cosmic functioning. *Function and Law were identified.*

Now, in reality, such functioning is not identified with the law *for* that functioning. There has been a lot of confusion at this point. Physicists will speak of their mathematical formulae as laws. But these formulae, of course, are not the Law for physical functions; they are shorthand symbolical formulations of the regular subjective responses or uniformities the physicist observes in physical situations. We cannot observe the Law directly; we observe it indirectly through observation of the lawful responses of things to the Law-demand. What the Law itself is we know from the Word of God.

Functionalism

The view that the only Law is the lawful behaviour observed in the states of affairs of things and persons we call *functionalism*. Here we have another one of those "ism" words. God created a cosmos of functions under the Law. The functional cosmos has its own place in the whole. But it is not also the Law. When one identifies the two he makes the functional cosmos to be "more" *in his theory* than it is *in reality* by virtue of God's creation-ordinance. The theory exaggerates *(distorts)* the place of the functional cosmos by enlarging its role. That is functionalism.

This functionalism appeared in the Greek world in two main types, because there are two different kinds of function of the cosmos. I can scarcely take the time to make this thoroughly clear. But we shall make a beginning now, and possibly return to it in one way or another tomorrow.

We have spoken a number of times of the great diversity of functional life we find in this temporal existence of ours: physical and organic, psychical and analytical, historical, lingual, economic, aesthetic, ethical and so on. Now, I can say, for example, that we men are so constituted that among other things we can sense what is beautiful. Seeing an accident on the street, I can point my finger and say that one of the parties was responsible. That is a kind of human experience, but I doubt if any of us would call it an *aesthetic* experience. But if you see me in an art gallery drinking in the beauty of the light on an old Rembrandt canvas you say that I am having an aesthetic experience. I can have the same experience by looking at the sunset, or by sitting and listening to a symphony or concerto on my hi-fi set. I am busy drinking in beauty. But now, also that Rembrandt and the concerto and the sunset are beautiful. They all, as I, function somehow in an aesthetic way. Aesthetic laws hold for those *objects* of my aesthetic appreciation as well as for my *subjective* appreciation itself.

Again, I am such a being that I can pledge my fidelity to my fellowman. Human society is unthinkable without this element of constancy, as the Greek philosophical comic poet Epicharmos pointed out in his criticism of the constantly changing man of Xenophanes. I make such a pledge of faithfulness when I take a life-partner, and I wear this wedding-ring as a symbol of that pledge. What now is that wedding-ring? You might take a look, and say that it's beautiful. To be sure, it functions aesthetically. You might also have said that it's a good example of technical construction. Again you are right. But you have not put your finger on the dominant function of the wedding-ring until you have pointed to its symbolizing *ethical* meaning, the faithfulness of man to man. Yet that wedding-ring does not function ethically in the same way I do; it does not, for example, go around pledging its troth. We say that man functions as an ethical *subject;* the ring, as an *ethical object.* But the object-function of the ring requires the corresponding human subject function. Created reality everywhere displays this subject-object structure.

Flowers do not function in a social way *subjectively:* they develop no forms of social intercourse. But when brought into the club room or reception hall they serve to heighten the subjective social life of man. They make it, for example, that the rooms "lend themselves better" to pleasant and easy social intercourse. In the social sphere they function *objectively.* Likewise, that gas and oil out there in the province of Alberta, tin, copper and iron all can function as *objects* in the technical, economic and aesthetic life of man. Water as a concrete thing you first think of as a physical and not an organic "thing" (although frequently there may be organic "things"—we would hope quite harmless—floating around in it). Yet we may never "shut off" water into a purely physical world of Matter. In the cosmos of God's creation it has an objective function in connection with organic life: water is necessary for the sustenance of that life. And who would wish to deny the psychical or "feeling" role it plays in our life when we crave the "feel" of one more late summer's dash into the surf?

Everywhere, on all the modal levels except the earliest (i.e. the numerical), we find these subject-object relationships in the functional cosmos. Now, when we group all the possible *subject*-functions of all the modal levels together, we have the *subjective* side of the functional cosmos. Similarly, we can group all the *object*-functions together and have the *objective* side of the functional cosmos.

Subjectivism and Objectivism, the two Forms of Functionalism

It is for this reason that in Greek philosophy functionalism could assume the two forms of *subjectivism* and *objectivism*. In each case the Law is identified with one side or the other of the functional cosmos. We must therefore always keep in mind that subjectivism and objectivism are not the same as subjective and objective. "Subjective" and "objective" refer to the two sides of the functional cosmos of God's creation; they belong to the true structure of reality. On the other hand, the terms "subjectivism" and "objectivism" (with their corresponding adjectives "subjectivistic" and "objectivistic") are only applicable to human theoretical constructions in which a greater ontic role is assigned to "the subjective" or "the objective", as the case may be, than these have in reality by reason of the Law-word of God. Subjectivism **raises** some subject-functioning to the status of Law, which function never has; objectivism does the same thing with some objective functioning.

It will help here to offer a brief example of subjectivism. In classical aesthetic theory there are laws coming from *without* which the aesthetic performer must look to and obey if his work is to be aesthetically good. But a truly romantic spirit will burst out: No; Mozart is his own Law. He need not look outside himself for a standard or norm; he himself and he alone is the Norm. Mozart's playing of the piano is the Law for piano-playing. The Genius is his own Law. Now that is subjectivism. Here is the identification of Law and subjective behaviour. The Kinsey report on the sexual behaviour of the American male is another example of the same thing: there is no Law except what the subject itself *does*.

Objectivism is a little different. The subjectivists had not yet learned to distinguish the difference between the two kinds of functioning: subject and object. The objectivists have, but they immediately proceed to identify their newly discovered object with the Law for the subject. You see at once: the objectivistic conception of the creation-order is *analytically richer;* it has seen in some fashion the difference there really *is* between subject and object; it has "probed" deeper into the rich diversity of God's creation. But we must not now make the mistake of rushing to call objectivism a *truer* conception than subjectivism. For the object is *not* the Law for the subject; nor is the subject related to the object as to its norm. The whole newly seen relationship is also seen *distortedly*. In reality both subject- and object-function are subject(ed) to the Law. The whole ontology of Greek objectivism, where even the gods are subject(ed) to the Object, is a gross distortion of the structure of reality. At work in the distortion is the religious need to say what the Law is. The advance in analysis is at once affected by this deeper religious factor. Thus a theory can be analytically richer and yet not one whit more true. (Remember what we said at the beginning of this lecture about the meaning of "truth".)

It is not difficult to see how the Greek objectivists, given their paganistic, immanentistic religious "bent", could mistake the object for the Law. For one thing, the Law is the firm foundation of everything. The whole creation is anchored in the surety (Dutch, de vastheid) of God's Law-word. These apostate men too are in need of that Security, that solid Ground, that Comfort of which the Heidelberg Catechism speaks, just as all of us men are. But they do not seek it where it is to be found; they seek it *within* created reality. And now, lo, this object they have just discovered as a new something distinct from the subject appears to these men to be that needed and sought for sure ground, much surer than mere subjective existence. For that reason they speak of it as "that which truly *is*," in contrast to the subjective as "that which not *is*", i.e. that which does not come up to the standard of *reliable being*.

A very brief illustration will suffice here. When on Monday morning we are told that the minister's wife ran away after the evening service with the most prominent elder of the congregation, we say, Why, I'd never have dreamed of such a thing; and I knew them both very well. How little we really know another human subject! Yes, there you have all the uncertainty that is involved in our knowledge of subjects. But now let me hold up before all of you here in this room a book in a red and black binding. Each one of you subjects responds that the binding is red and black. That seems so sure to you that you would mark as abnormal anyone who did not agree. And your knowledge of those colours would seem to *remain* sure day after day. Now the natural *subjects* (fruit juices or whatever) that were used for the colors are one thing, and our knowledge of them may be highly uncertain; the color that I sense is a psychical object-function of those subjects, related to my psychical functioning as subject. And *that object seems really knowable and really reliable.*

A second factor present in the situation we have just described and further abetting the confusion of object and Law is that the object exercises a tremendous influence upon my subjective behaviour. Did we not all feel *compelled* just now to say that the cover of the book was red and black? That's the law on that subject; that judgment on our part would seem to be *binding.* But is it not the work of the Law to bind? The famous Socrates of Greek philosophy was an objectivist. It seems he did a good deal of thinking about man's technical work, and the role of the technical object especially impressed him. An artisan must know his materials, and what they lend themselves for. He would not think of making shoes out of marble, or statues of leather. The object determines what the subject can do and what he does. Just think how much our conduct is governed by all the sights, smells, sounds and tastes of our daily experience!

Whatever is right in all this analysis of the role of the object, there is something badly wrong about it too. The role of the object has been confused with the role of the Law. Your girl may decide that she *wants you*. She wears an alluring perfume, and you find yourself very much subject to its influence. No doubt it will influence your behaviour. But it is not the *Norm* for your behaviour. Objects undoubtedly govern our conduct in many ways; they are not the Law for them. And if we confuse the role of object and the role of Law we may find ourselves in serious trouble.

Platonic Realism

It was Plato who finally came to realize that the Law is not to be found in any subject- or object-functioning. He recognized both subjects and objects; he granted the subject-object relation. But the Law was a third thing. The Law was a separate realm of law-essences. This Greek ontological view we call *realism*. It is the third of the distorting Greek views about the Law.

In this Platonic realism we once more find *analytical advance that does not bring us one whit closer to the Truth*. (Remember what we have been saying about the Truth.) It is, of course, *correct* to say, as Plato does, that the Law is not something within the cosmos of functions. But Plato does not say that because, being in the grip of the Word of God, he knows the Truth about the Law. His negative statement is yet abstract until you hear why he says that. Analytically, Plato has found difficulties with identifying the Law with any functions. But that does not bring him to the Truth about the Law. *For the Truth cannot be found analytically.* Without the revealing POWER of the Word of God Plato can only use his analytical results in the service of one more religious distortion. And that is what his realism is.

Plato taught a separate world of law-essences, of *things* that are at one and the same time *abiding and sure principles of oughtness* (even more sure than the Object of the objectivists) and *perfect, eternal models* of all earthly forms of existence. I am speaking of Plato's world of *ideas*. In this other world we find, for instance, what it is for the good to be, or the *law for the good*. But this law is itself a perfect Thing, a Substance: it is the Good Itself. Likewise, we find there what it is for the beautiful to be, or the *law for the beautiful*. But again, the law is also a Thing: the Beautiful Itself. And so also we find in this world of ideas Man Himself (the law for what it is to be man), Circle Itself, even Numbers Themselves (e.g. Seven Itself), etc.

These law-essences are law substances that simply subsist in the cosmos and have the force of law. Gods and men are subject to them. They are called purely intelligible essences, which means that they are beheld by Mind alone and not by the changing senses (which are admixed with something not rational). It is right at this point that we see the apostate character of Platonic realism. Really to know the *Law* is to tremble before the God of the whole earth, Whose word the Law is. In Plato the law has been divorced from the sovereign God; it exists in itself. It is *substance*. And it is intelligible substance. That is, with all the supposed calmness and self-possession of normalcy I simply look out with my Mind toward a realm of eternally-existent, purely intelligible law-essences and behold the Truth. All the "fear and trembling" has been removed. And it is not the religious depth-relation to God that is necessary here to know the Law and the Truth, but only our rational life, elevated to the heart-position. The veritable Truth of God, that Reality is the Covenant of Life between man and God, has been utterly lost sight of. Whatever may be correct and "noble" in Plato's analysis, we have to do in his philosophy primarily with the falsity of apostasy. Plato, fallen from his representative Place (Office) in the cosmos, cannot "see" the nature of the Truth.

The Christian Thesis

This account we have now so summarily given will have to suffice to illustrate the nature of antithetical thought. I think we can all see a lot better now that it is the Word of God that alone grants to us men the Light of Truth, and that without it, even though we are forever dealing, as we *must*, with the Law-order of the **Creator-God, we can** never arrive at a knowledge of the Truth. The religious situation of man demands a repressing and supplanting Distortion, the Lie, to take the place of the Truth that is being repressed.

I believe that one last thing ought yet to be said by way of clarifying this matter of antithesis before we close. Many of us are, I am sure, inclined to think of the *Christian* side of the struggle with the world of unbelief as the *antithetical* side. We sometimes hear the Christian position spoken of as the position of the Antithesis. That can only mean, however, that the struggle of the Kingdom of Christ is in *antithetical relation* to the struggle of the Kingdom of Darkness. In our thinking about the matter we must never lose sight of what is *prior*. The creation-order, firmly secured in the Divine Will, is the Original Truth. And the Christian religion is in very truth the re-proclamation, in the Second Representative (Office-bearing) Man, of the Order of Creation, centered in the covenantal life-fellowship of God and man. God's righteousness in Christ (Romans 1) calls us back to Life in terms of the Law-order. Christ, as we saw, brings us back to the creation- ordinances. As such, Christianity is the re-proclamation of the THESIS. God's Truth is first. The repressing and supplanting Distortion, the LIE or ANTITHESIS, came second, and *on the human level,* and can only exist as a distortion of (thus dependent upon) the THESIS. The Word of God is the POWER that liberates us from the Darkness of the LIE that has darkened the insight of our race (see Job) and sets us in the Light of Truth. The certainty of the Truth is not our work. All certitude is the work of the Word and Spirit of God in our hearts. Let us bless the Word of God always.

Lecture III

Synthesis

Before I get into the material of this last lecture I want to say a word of appreciation to all you participants in this Unionville Study Conference. I spoke in the first lecture of a certain hesitation in Canada as to the way we have to go, but I must say that my contacts with you students here, and with the teachers and the ministers of the gospel, have caused me to think that the hesitation is somewhat less than I had supposed. At least in some very promising places. At any rate, the spirit in this Conference is wonderful. I just had to say to you that I am really overwhelmed, thankful to God and happy about the spirit everywhere present here.

The Thread of the Lectures

Now, we have talked together so far about *Thesis* and *Antithesis,* and today we must make an effort to understand what is meant by *Synthesis*. But for just a moment yet you will have to be patient with me while I pick up the main thread of the lectures for one more time, and say a couple of things that really have to be said before we come to this question of synthesis itself.

The first thing I want to say this morning is that I am quite sure that yesterday's lecture was more difficult than today's will be. That is a good idea, is it not, to shove the most difficult lecture into the middle position, where it is nicely hidden away? I suppose some people will think it unwise that I have attempted so much in these lectures. I can only plead that I quite deliberately chose to do it this way. I do not, of course, expect you in these three days to get a firm grasp on everything I have said. We do not, unfortunately for me, have the opportunity to talk frequently together about these great central matters of our life; for that reason we must choose those things which, lying at the very heart, determine all the rest. All I can hope is that somewhere deep in your selfhood you will sense, in general, *the lay of the land as a whole*. That is what you need first, I believe: a general sense of the lay of the whole land; some sense of the *direction* our work as Christians ought to take in general. I am myself very much convinced that everything in the world of learning depends on the *point of departure* of one's thought. And that all problems light up in their true meaning *when seen from out of the centre*. Always there is the question of totality-structure, of Order. It governs the fundamental formulations of every special science. And so I have chosen the material for these lectures in this way. It may be a little harder on all of us. But I am thinking first of all of the new direction it can give to all our work in the coming years, as we go on individually and collectively in our human calling. From what we shall have done together here you will find, I think, that you can go on and read the books —a great variety of them—more quickly, more efficiently, grasp their big ideas more thoroughly, conduct your discussions with each other more fruitfully, and so on.

In the two previous lectures I tried to suggest that our awareness of the totality-structure of reality is not some knowledge *analytically* arrived at on our part, but is *heart*-knowledge, the result of the work of God's Word upon our hearts. We said that by His Word God grasps hold of us in the religious centre of our existence and sets us in the Truth. The Word of God is thus seen to be the Word of Truth, and we can now see *the intrinsic relation it bears to the world of learning,* the problem that beckoned in our first lecture. The Truth of the Word of God is fortunately not just the simple proclamation: JESUS SAVES. It is, in very truth, the re-proclamation of that creation-order that is centered in the basic religious relation between man and God. In an integral creation-order thus centered, the Fall of *man* meant the radical falling away of the *entire creation* from its religious concentration upon God. The Restoration is therefore a radical restoration of the entire creation to its directedness upon the loving and obedient service of God through the heart of man. Thus the Word as re-proclamation is re-proclamation in terms of the New Head of the creation, the Saviour Jesus Christ. *But we must never see God or Christ or man apart from the Law-order of God.* God, Self and Law-order are always together. Just as God is the absolute Origin of the entire creation (and there is thus nothing left over beside Him), so within the order of creation God finds His creaturely image in the heart of man, the concentration-point of all the aspects of meaning of temporal reality.[1] There can thus be no two-ness (or three-ness) of substantial "parts" in man: the *whole man,* in *all* his temporal aspects and relations, is in the scriptural view integrally (without any remnant) directed in the religious centre of his being towards God and is there concentrated on the whole-hearted service which is the fulfilling of the Law. But now, further, God had made man the *lord of creation.* Thus the whole creation too, whatever diversity of moments it displays in a temporal way, exists only in relation to man and in him is gathered up in the integral religious meaning. The temporal creation then is also an *integral order,* and not, for example, a world of Matter and a world of Mind. It is impossible to think of some *aspect* of the integral creation-order as existing by itself as a separate "world", a special "world" of matter, for instance. In the midst of the world as we *concretely* experience it stands man. Any effort to conceive a separate world of matter involves human thought and language: every *concept* of natural phenomena implies *human conceiving,* expressed in mathematical formulae, etc. To get from the concrete world as it is with us in the midst of it to an abstract concept of 'Nature' requires abstraction, and that very abstraction is a logical-theoretical activity that presupposes man and his thinking. So there we are again with man very much involved at the heart of things.

Greek Thought as Antithesis of Truth

We saw yesterday how in the apostate world of (Greek) thought this integral character of all reality had been lost to view. Lacking the central religious knowledge of the selfhood that only the Word of God can implant within us, the Greeks had to fill up the lacuna of this religious knowledge by *enlarging* (absolutizing) one of the relative aspects of the temporal order and elevating it to the central religious place of the heart. It is the True nature of things (that man is heart) that drove the Greeks

---

[1] Here one would do well to read the excellent lectures entitled "What Is Man?" in the volume Dooyeweerd, *In The Twilight of Western Thought,* Philadelphia, 1960.

of necessity to their *religious distortion of what they analytically find* in their experience of this temporal life. You realize, of course, that this is true of all apostate men, and not only of the Greeks. But in the Greek world we find the beginnings of mighty historical traditions that have influenced men in all later ages to apply certain principles of total-structuration in their analysis of their experiences. These principles we found to be pseudo-principles, the Distortion, the LIE, that must arise in the religious repression and supplanting of the TRUTH. They are not of an *analytical* character, and we shall never be able to get at and deal with what is really taking place here in men's lives if we insist on thinking of them as such, that is, as rational achievements on their part.

We saw, further, yesterday that a diversity, actually quite a wide diversity, of such pseudo-principles of total-structuration has arisen in the course of philosophical speculation. (Mankind is a religious fellowship or Community in the Truth that is wrought by the Spirit of God.) Lacking the Truth (the central and integral religious meaning of the totality of the several aspects of temporal reality), apostate men have turned first to one and then to another of these temporal *aspects* of the central religious meaning of the creation. I want to say one more thing about this before we go any further. I think you will find it worth while to take a somewhat closer look at this phenomenon of the *diversity of schools*. For whether we work in mathematics, in psychology, in logic, in the language sciences, social sciences or any other special area we shall always be confronted with this *diversity of schools of interpretation* of the field of investigation. It is the question of the *point of view:* where one must stand to oversee the entire field *aright*.

Schools of interpretation arise from this tendency. Men have to take one particular *aspect* of created reality for the whole of it, thereby reducing all the other aspects to so many *modes* of the one they have just thus absolutized. But now, to take a relative aspect, imbedded as it is in a whole scale of similarly relative aspects, and religiously to absolutize it and make all the others relative to it as their *fulness of meaning*—that is not just to make an error here or there in one's reasoning; that is to obscure one's view of the whole structure of reality. For then one can no longer grasp *any one* of the aspects in its peculiar inner nature. One has then the Lie, an untrue view of the totality.

Real Basis for all the 'Isms'

How is it possible to be in such a position and still show signs of being sufficiently in touch with reality to uncover, as scientists do, even important *moments* of truth (those fairly correct statements about limited states of affairs that constantly press upon us all)?

The answer lies, in part, in the inner structure of the several aspects themselves. No aspect is a thing cut off from the other aspects; in each aspect we find a *modal expression of the integral and radical character of created reality*[1]*:* There is, for instance, the psychical aspect of feeling: a specific sphere of functions subject to their own laws. In the *irreducibility* of the psychical to any other aspect we have what we call its *sphere-sovereignty*. But over against that there is the principle of *sphere-universality*. For the one aspect cannot even *be* except in indissoluble coherence with all the other aspects that together make up the integral whole of reality. Thus we find within 'the psychical' what we call a feeling-*life*. Now, *feeling*-life is not primary or organic *life;* it is rather an analogy or mirroring of the aspect of life within the psychical, in a psychical sense. Likewise, emotion or the movement of feeling is a mirroring of physical-chemical *movement,* but within the psychical, in a psychical sense. We could all distinguish within the psychical, further, *logical* feeling, feeling for *language* (taalgevoel), aesthetic feeling, ethical feeling, feeling of reverence or awe before God, etc. All these feelings show the intimate connection of the psychical with all the other aspects of our temporal existence.

Or take 'the aesthetic' aspect of a concrete aesthetic production. Can you imagine a painting or a symphony without a *number* of parts? Yet *that* number is not primary number, the numerical aspect of the creation-order; it is an *aesthetic mirroring* of the aspect of number: the parts are *aesthetic* parts. There must also be aesthetic space and movement (spread out, compressed, metres, rhythms, etc.). If I had time I could show how every other aspect is mirrored within 'the aesthetic'.

This creation-principle of sphere-universality is no doubt

---

[1] See Dooyeweerd, *Transcendental Problems of Philosophic Thought*, pp. 42-48.

what has supplied whatever grounds men have been able to adduce for their attempts to find the whole meaning of reality in what is actually but one aspect. But of course *the mirroring of all the sides is not the same thing as all the sides.* It is here therefore that all the "isms"—materialism, organicism, psychologism, logicism, technicism, economism, historicism, aestheticism, moralism, etc.—arise, find a specious legitimacy, but ultimately flounder. Each seems to have something to say for itself; each is in fact a *religious* distortion of the fulness of meaning of reality.

And when you think that we can distinguish at least fourteen or fifteen aspects, you can see what a variety of interpretation is "possible" here. Further—remembering what we discussed yesterday—there is the possibility of overemphasizing either the subject-side (subjectivism) or the object-side (objectivism) or even the law-side (realism) of all these various modal aspects. Hence, the great and confusing array of philosophical "schools" that have repeatedly taken possession of the hearts of men and tried to keep men *satisfied apart from a knowledge of the Truth.*

The Attempt at Synthesis

It is time to be getting on to the subject of today's lecture. Thesis and Antithesis, we have now seen, are actually related to each other as the total Truth to the total distorting Lie. Two things so related can never be accommodated to each other, can never be brought to mutual adjustment. Yet it is just that that is attempted in *Synthesis.*

Synthesis, then, is the attempt to combine the Truth of the Word of God with the constructions of thought that have arisen in the apostate mind. You need only recall that many church fathers of the first Christian centuries had, previous to their conversion to Christianity, been trained in one or another of the philosophical "schools" of thought of the ancient world, some quite thoroughly. Their subsequent "reading" of the Word of God often suffered from the fact that apostate thought had already taken strong hold upon their hearts: they had grown accustomed to looking upon themselves, the world and even God in a certain way, in a way that was actually in conflict with the Truth of God. Yet in one way or another the several fathers of the church tried to "harmonize" the Scriptures and their previously acquired "view". In this way, often perhaps somewhat unintentionally, the POWER of the Word of God was removed by forcing "elements" of biblical truth into structures of thought that, alien to the "elements", put upon these another meaning than they have in the Word itself. The integral radical character of the creation was lost to view; the central religious situation of man was obscured; true religion was weakened.

If those early fathers had clearly seen what the Word of God really is, and thus seen its *intrinsic relation to the world of learning,* they would undoubtedly have seen also that synthesis is impossible. For there are no *biblical "elements"* apart from the *one structure* of the Word of God, the Truth. Neither are there "elements" of pagan thought that are not "in-formed" by the deep-seated apostatic principles of total-structuration that distort the *whole.* The warfare between the Truth of God and the distorting Lie of religious repression is a *total* one that is found everywhere among the "details" of our analytical life, underlying these. Synthesis is thus seen to be an utter impossibility; men can *attempt* it, but they cannot consummate it. And the inner tension between the two alien religious basic-motives drives men on to a Choice. For that reason the modern period of history has, except in traditionalistic "orthodox" Christian circles, rejected the attempt as even an acceptable ideal: modern thought is decidedly anti-synthetic. You can see now why I had in these lectures to begin with a discussion of the nature and role of the Word of God. When you see what that is, your position is decided. You will reject all efforts at synthesis. (This does not mean, of course, that we are not forever finding ourselves *guilty* of making synthetic attempts. We are sinners not yet wholly subject to the Rule of the Word. But we will recognize our *guilt* and reject the desirability of synthesis when we have seen the nature of the Word of God.)

Law as Rational a priori and its Synthesis with Revelation about Law of God

Synthetic philosophical conceptions can be just about as manifold as the number of apostate conceptions. For one could attempt to understand the Word of God in the "light" of any one of the traditional Greek conceptions (except perhaps materialism). In these lectures it is naturally impossible for me to go into all the possibilities. Instead, I choose one line of attempt at synthesis and go into it somewhat more fully. This one I choose has to do with a synthesis of the Word and a certain pagan view of the Law. We have seen how fundamental the Law is. This particular story I am choosing had, further, the most momentous consequences for our modern life. If you Canadian students are to understand your new homeland and its universities, an inquiry into this particular history that I am about to relate is quite indispensable.

To begin the story I must get back once more to the ancient world. The Law, you must remember, *holds for* created reality. All men, even though fallen away from a knowledge of the Truth, necessarily experience the *influence* of the Law. But pagan men cannot know what the Law is; for it is nothing else than the Will of the sovereign God for His creation. Not knowing what it is, but experiencing it as a real power in their life, the Greeks were driven to a distorted account of it. Thus far I have shown you three Greek answers to the question about the nature of the Law: subjectivism, objectivism and realism.

Ultimately there came a *fourth answer*, and it is to it that I wish to limit myself now. This view arose not in the classical Greek age (which we may conveniently consider as coming to a close with the deaths of Alexander the Great and Aristotle in 323 and 322 B.C. respectively), but in the following *Hellenistic period*. From that time it entered into many aspects of the work of church fathers, medieval scholastic philosophers and church canonists, and finally experienced a mighty resurgence in the great revival of Stoical ideas of the seventeenth century, when it became the veritable mainspring of modern political and social action. (Ernst Cassirer has a fine chapter, "The Renaissance of Stoicism and 'Natural Right' Theories of the State", ch. XIII of his important book *The Myth of the State*.)

This fourth view about the Law we call the theory of the *a priori*. Although I have indirectly intimated (by the reference to Cassirer's book) that it is connected with the Stoics, it is in actuality not restricted to them, but emerges in one form or another in just about every philosophical "school" of the Hellenistic period, each time as the result of a certain analogous development that is taking place in the several "schools". Prof. Vollenhoven of the Free University of Amsterdam has done wonderful historical pioneer work on this question.

Speaking very generally, we can describe what took place as follows. The new, frequently non-Greek, peoples who now begin to appear upon the philosophical stage become skeptical of (i.e. they call into question) the — to them — dogmatical pronouncements of their Greek predecessors. Now those "pronouncements" had concerned in the first instance whatever in a given philosophical conception was taken to be the *ground of certainty*, that which supposedly was *eminently knowable*. And that, of course, has to do with the Law. In objectivism it was the Object (the capital letter suggesting the exaggeration of object to Law); in realism, the law-essences or absolute Substances. The Hellenistic Age is characterized in philosophical matters first of all by the *skeptical movement,* which in each "school" calls into question first the eminent knowability and thereafter the very existence of whatever in the school is being taken as the Law.

To imagine the effect of this scepsis you need only remember that the Object, for the objectivist, and the ideas (law-essences), for the realist, are the *Guide of life.* Think of Socrates 'analysis of handicraft: the artisan is guided by what the objective material lends itself for. The Object of the objectivist *directs* my subjective functioning ("affects" and "is law for" have been confused here, you will remember); the ideas of Plato are the Truth by which our lives are to be directed. With the rise of the scepsis, doubt has now arisen with respect to these several Guides of life.

The Emphasis on the Subjective

In the course of the Hellenistic centuries we see in all the philosophical schools a solution gradually being worked out to meet the new need for certainty in life. The solution almost universally accepted is the theme of the *a priori*. This new theme says, in effect, that the certainty, the direction I need in my life but no longer have from any external Object or world of law-essences *I have within myself*. The Mesoplatonists (a post-scepsis development in the Academy that Plato had founded), for instance, said something like this: the ideas of Plato, as criteria for the true, the good and the beautiful, simply cannot be missed; life as it must be lived requires some *principial direction* from the beginning, some *directing knowledge;* if my life is not to be direction-less and meaningless, there simply have to be such absolute Norms as Plato had conceived in the ideas. These Mesoplatonists then went on *to agree with their sceptical predecessors* in the Academy (the Middle and New Academy) that the ideas do not exist where Plato had looked for them, viz. in a separate world behind this world of process, *but also to add* that exist they do, and that *in our own thinking mind* (the Nous).

From this we see the true nature of this theme of the *a priori*. The Law of God is the Firm Foundation of the creation, the Director of our ways. As the Word that faithfully establishes His covenant with us, the Law is also our only Comfort. The earlier pagans lacked this central religious certainty. But as religious creatures they need and seek something that can take the place of this Law-word of God. They had sought this Basis and Director of Life in Nature, in the Object, in a separate world of law-essences (ideas). But now in this new theme of the *a priori,* they seek it *within their own subjective knowledge-possession*. The Law is no longer looked upon as something extra-mental, about which extra-mental knowledge can be acquired in the form of concepts, judgments, etc., but as something that itself is a *concept,* thus *knowledge*. Of course, it is not a concept like other concepts: it is not only a *universal* concept but also a *binding* concept (one having the force of law). Such a concept is not, like other concepts, due to experience (i.e. it does not arise out of experience), but *precedes every possible experience and constitutes* experience (as to its lawful structure). It is a *concept a priori*. It is *knowledge a priori. Innate ideas*.

The illustration has been used of the "sensitive jelly glass". Here is a jelly glass just like other jelly glasses in most respects, only this one was "sensitive". Each year, this sensitive jelly glass once mused to itself, the housewife prepared various sorts of jellies, and finally placed these in the various jelly glasses. But at this point the sensitive jelly glass was confronted with a problem. One year its contents had been green and thin; another year, thicker and red, and so on. But every year the *shape*, the *form* of the contents had been the very same. And now this sensitive jelly glass, after some further "musing", came up with the solution: the *color* and *consistency* of the contents had come from the contents that had been poured in; the *form or shape* of the contents, however, must be due to the nature of the jelly glass itself. The jelly glass' own nature determined, as the *a priori*, the possibility of the form. So our minds, possessed of the *a priori* law (the Truth), determine the possibilities of our life.

The Concept of Reason

Here is the origin of that concept of "Reason" that looms so large and exercises so fundamental and pervasive an influence in the modern rationalistic philosophy of western Europe from the seventeenth through the nineteenth centuries. "Reason" does not exist; there is no such thing. Incidentally, that is why we may never give an answer to the question, What is the relation of faith and reason? The question is not properly formulated. God endowed us at the creation with *understanding;* "Reason" is that understanding *distorted* in apostate theory by being "enlarged" to include the Law as *a priori knowledge-content* (the Truth). In the Distortion "Reason", instead of the Word of God, becomes the Principle, the Director, the Guide of life, the Source of Truth. Already you begin to discern the modern chant: Reason, the only Oracle of man. Arrived at this point we can see ahead to the *lumen naturale* of Descartes, the 'natural light'. That 'natural light', instead of being the Light which the creation-order is as *revelation* (which revelation man in apostasy is not in a position to receive as light but must repress and thus remain in darkness), has turned into an *inner light of each man's deepest Self, a light capable of directing him through to final salvation, and that apart from the efficacious application to him by God's Spirit of the redemption purchased by Christ.*

It is accordingly not difficult to see that the concept of Reason belongs to the realm of apostate Antithesis, is a concept of Truth in *antithetical relation* to the Truth and Light of the Divine Word. Yet you will be disappointed if you expect your Anglo-Saxon neighbour to see that. Is that a mystery? Then let me clear away the mystery at once by saying that it is not some virtue in Dutchmen and some lack in Anglo-Saxon blood that makes the difference. To understand the U.S.A. and Canada (or Australia or New Zealand), to understand much that you will hear in your university classes and in all this particular intellectual world around us here you will have to know something about the devastating role that *synthesis-thinking* has played in Christian circles, also in connection with this theme of the *a priori*. In the Netherlands the appearance on the scene of Groen van Prinsterer, Kuyper, the philosophy of the Law-idea *(de Wijsbegeerte der Wetsidee)*, etc. signalled a desire for a radical break with long-established patterns of synthesis-thinking in favour of a radically scriptural outlook upon and approach to life. That is what has made Dutch Calvinism distinctive; that has been the strength of the revival of Christian life and scholarship in the Netherlands. For the Word of God is the only POWER that can re-direct man's ways to blessedness in covenantal fellowship with God. In other Protestant countries the integral strength of living by the Scriptures has constantly been sapped by the hold that synthesis-thinking has had upon the hearts of men.

The Choice Before Us Today

This is the situation that I was describing at the beginning of the first lecture. We have to choose which way we are going to go in Canada. Also in our scholarship. It is the choice between a way radically (i.e. from out of the root or centre of our existence) and thus exclusively directed by Scripture and a way that seeks a synthesis between the Truth of the Word of God and the Lie of apostasy. The absolutely fundamental importance of this question for you and me individually, for the whole fabric of our life together as Christians in the future, and even for the prospect of evangelizing this north American continent in any *integral sense*, requires that I take a little time, in the remainder of this lecture, to show you the nature of synthesis-thinking.

We can, I think, best begin with the case of Justin Martyr. This man was a typical Hellenistic wandering philosopher. He had been born in Palestine early in the second century after Christ, had been subject to Platonic, Stoical and other Hellenistic philosophical influences, and finally had become a Christian about A.D. 133, probably at Ephesus. He was martyred at Rome ca. 165.

Synthesis in Justin Martyr

Justin's acquaintance with the philosophical movements of his time would certainly have introduced him to the widely held theme of the *a priori*. But let us see what he does with it after he has become a Christian. The name of Justin is connected with what is called the *logos-speculation*. 'Logos,' as you may know, is the Greek word that occurs at the beginning of John's gospel and is translated "Word". "In the beginning was the Word," etc. In Greek *'logos'* means not only *"word"* but also *"reason"*. In the writings of Justin and other early Christian apologists the concepts of Reason (natural light, or natural revelation *experienced as light*, i.e. not repressed by a sinful heart, revelation that *gets home* and directs us to our ultimate salvation) and of the Word are confused, and appeal is typically made to such a verse as John 1:9. At that place we read, "That was the true light, which lighteth every man that cometh into the world". That, at least, is the translation you will find in the King James Version. Actually, the words "that cometh" are a present participle in Greek ("coming") in a form that would allow as antecedent either the word "light" or the word "man". But Justin and others apparently took the verse to mean that Christ as the light of Reason illumines the rational processes of all men as they are born into the world. This He does apparently not particularly as Redeemer but as the agent of creation. For the operation of the one Logos is apparent everywhere; *universally* He sets our minds right in their law-concepts (the *a priori*) as to the good, the true and the beautiful. Whoever had permitted the seed-corn to germinate in his soul and had lived according to the directions of the logos Christians counted as *one of themselves,* i.e. men like Herakleitos, Sokrates and the Stoic Musonius. Justin says the Stoics and others were able to speak of a logos in their philosophy only because they were themselves illumined by the Logos, whom Christians *know* in Christ. In his effort to get the ear of the emperor and to win his old pagan associates Justin would show the *essential unity* of *truth* in Greek philosophy *and* the divine revelation *specially* in Scripture. *The antithesis between true and false prophecy is concealed behind an assumed mere difference of degree of clarity of insight. That is synthesis.*

Hans Lietzmann writes in his *The Founding of the Church Universal* (p. 239): "(The Logos) became the 'new law-giver', although the 'new, eternal, and final' law was the old law of rational virtue long recognized by sages". Again (p. 240): "Christianity of this kind was a genuinely philosophical reconstruction built of familiar elements. The idea of God was borrowed from popular philosophy and, even in the expressions employed, corresponded with what we can find among the religious-minded

Stoics in the first century . . . . Already in John's Gospel, Jesus Christ had been described as the *logos* of God. Whereas in John, this identification was meant to abrogate the historical limitations of Jesus' life and to raise it to eternal significance, we find in Justin a tendency almost in the contrary direction. The purpose was to render it impossible to reject the authority of Christ's teaching in this way, and to make it cast a light on the examination conducted by reason. Jesus was indeed the incarnate divine reason, and consequently everything truly reasonable on this earth must in the end agree with Christianity."

There is one more sentence I must cite from Lietzmann (p. 241): ". . . in whatever ways this doctrine may have penetrated in detail into Justin's working ideas and however strange it may seem when contrasted with the early Christian ideas, Justin and his fellow-warriors introduced it into speculative theology, placed it immediately on the throne, where it kept its place victoriously for many centuries". There you have the <u>historical influence</u> of <u>synthesis-thought.</u> And let me append at once, as illustration of the continued sway of these ideas, the words F. Godet comments upon John 1:9 in his widely-used Commentary: "It is more natural . . . to find here . . .the notion (of) the *Logos*, as the internal light, enlightening every man, illuminating him by the sublime intuitions of the good, the beautiful and the true". While on the very same page just before that he holds that these words signify "that the light of the *Logos* is a divine gift which every man brings with him when he is born—that the matter in question is, accordingly, an *innate* light" (italics mine). Godet knows the tradition. He writes (on verse 4 and the word Light): "All the rays of the sentiment of the beautiful, the true and the just which have illuminated and which ennoble humanity, justify the expression of John. It is this fundamental truth which was formulated by the Fathers (Justin, Clement of Alexandria) in their doctrine of the *logos spermatikos.*"

Synthesis in Later Christian Thought

We could go on. I should like to show you similar things in the greatest of the church fathers, Augustine of Hippo. You know, it is always particularly instructive to attend closely to Augustine. No father of the church understood better the central thrust of the Word of God. But, you know, we often make ourselves guilty of idealizing Augustine. Time after time, in his wrestling for the Truth, one can see how the deeply intrenched themes of pagan philosophy prevent his realizing fully what in a sense he understands of the Word of God. The theme of the *a priori*, combined with the theme of macrocosm and microcosm, a Greek conception of "soul" and "body", and much more that cannot be reconciled with the divine Word is to be found prominently exposed in the thought of Augustine. It is true that as he matured in the Christian faith, and particularly after he was made bishop, Augustine saw more and more the need of being "normed" exclusively by the Scriptures. The *Retractationes* speak eloquently here. Nevertheless, we ought never to give in to the *parole* of some quarters that we might well call ourselves Augustinians. Calvin is farther along the road of reformation than Augustine, and the line on to Kuyper and our own time is clear enough to the serious student who will investigate the matter. (Permit me to suggest the article "Kuyper's Wetenschapsleer" by Prof. Dooyeweerd in *Philosophia Reformata*, 1939.) We cannot turn the clock back; anachronism always ends in destruction of some kind. *For reformation is not to be found on the horizontal line; it is found in the vertical relation of obedience to the Word.*

I should like to have said something about the Nature-Grace scheme of Thomas Aquinas and the mighty scholastic movement in general, which has revived to become quite a power in the twentieth century. [You are well acquainted with the Pontifical Institute of Higher Studies here in Toronto.] And to have shown how a whole block of pagan thought (largely Aristotle's, plus a little platonism or neoplatonism and some stoicism) was thus allowed to remain intact, un-reformed by the central thrust of the Word of God. But time is now pressing, and I want, in conclusion, to bring up two particular synthetic movements that are of especially great importance for understanding the intellectual and religious climate of the North American continent. I refer to the Cambridge Platonists and the Scottish realists.

You must remember that we are here discussing these movements as examples of synthesis-thinking. To do that really effectively I would have to sketch for you something more of the revival of the apostate theme of the *a priori* in the seventeenth century. I have already referred to Descartes' 'natural light'. Time will allow me only to mention in passing the *De Veritate* (1624) of Herbert of Cherbury and the *De jure belli et pacis* (1625) of

Hugo Grotius. I have discussed their significance a bit in my Calgary paper of 1957, "The Development of Calvinism in North America on the Background of its Development in Europe", which has been used in the discussion of this problem by the Groen van Prinsterer Society at Calvin College.

The Approach of the Cambridge Platonists

Most of these Cambridge Platonists had had a Puritan bringing-up. One of the best recent books about them is that by the great German Jewish philosopher who came to the U.S.A. during the Second World War, Ernst Cassirer, *The Platonic Renaissance in England* (Thomas Nelson, 1953). More recently a volume was published by the Cambridge University Press showing the close connection between the Cambridge Platonists and the Remonstrants: R. L. Colie, *Light and Enlightenment,* a study of the Cambridge Platonists and the Dutch Arminians, 1957. What characterizes the teaching of this group of men?

They were moderates, taking up a position midway between the Puritans and the Prelatists. They were pleaders for toleration in the midst of England's civil wars. (See my Calgary paper for the significance of the modern concept of toleration.) But what is most characteristic of them is the way they deliberately founded their position on tolerance on a philosophic basis. That philosophic basis is their doctrine of the place of Reason in religion! They subordinate religious conviction to the law of sufficient reason. "Though the human mind is dependent on revelation for the full reality of the saving truths, yet it remains, nevertheless, the measure of their possibility." (Cassirer) These men had as their motto Proverbs 20:27: "The spirit of a Man is the Candle of the Lord", but they took that spirit to be Reason. "Reason *discovers* what is Natural; and Reason *receives* what is Supernatural", is how one of them puts it. "To go against Reason is to go against God" (Whichcote). Cassirer warns us rightly to bear in mind that "that reason upon which they would base religious faith is rather practical reason than theoretical reason. The *a priori* of pure morality is the starting-point of their doctrine; and from here they ascend to religious belief on the one hand, and on the other to the sphere of metaphysical certainty. To speculative knowledge of the nature of the soul and of the intelligible world." (p. 41)

To Puritans and Prelatists alike they say: Unite on essentials and agree to differ on non-essentials. But how does a man distinguish between these two? By improvement of one's reason, by its employment in the fields of science and of moral conduct, and above all, by its employment about the truths of Natural Religion. In this way one grows in knowledge of that which is most knowable of God—a process by which one becomes more and more "like unto God", till the perfection of reason is reached in that "Divine sagacity", as Henry More calls it, that "nativity from above" as Whichcote (the founder of the movement) calls it, which makes a man at last a sure judge of what is essential in the teaching of the Scriptures. The Cambridge Platonists go really farther than the Arminians. Reason must be sublimated or deified into "Divine sagacity" by the presence of God in the soul. The interpreter of inspired Scripture must be himself inspired. "Reason is the divine governor of man's life; it is the very voice of God".

Practical Effects of Cambridge Platonist Teaching

I think I need not take the pains to point out to you how the Truth of the Word of God is being distorted here by being accommodated to the idea of Reason as the Oracle of man. One practical effect of the teachings of these Cambridge Platonists I must not neglect to point out to you, however. Let me do it by citing something Prof. Martineau wrote in his *Types of Ethical Theory*, vol. II. p. 446 about one of these platonists, viz. Ralph Cudworth. "The 'Intelligible Ideas', then, are eternal and necessary modes of the divine mind; and from the infinite seat they pass into the finite world in two distinct, yet related ways: by an act of God's *Will*, things are called into existence of which they became the essences; by a lending of *His Spirit* to centres of dependent being, and communication of *His Consciousness*, they become the intuitive lights of reason and Conscience for all free natures: and thus, they guide us, on one line, to the true reading of the universe; and on the other, to the immediate sympathy of God. Hence it is that all men have the same fundamental ideas, to form the common ground both of intellectual communion and of moral Co-operation." That last sentence is basic. There we see how the synthesis of Christian ideas with the theme of the *a priori*, with the rationalistic dogma of the *commonness of Reason*, lays the groundwork for the modern secular belief in the possibility of

Community apart from a common allegiance to the Rule of Christ. Here we have the major historical factor in the rise of an Enlightenment idea of human society based on a common Reason. Here we have the explanation of the strong American faith in the common community undertakings, and the abhorrence of all specifically Christian social and political actions. It is not difficult to see that we are here well on the way to the Enlightenment deification of human reason, to its religion of reason, which was nothing more than a supposedly pure morality, i.e. morality without religion, and to its confident reliance upon *civic* virtues and *civic* institutions and *civic* education. The painful thing to realize is that movements in the Christian Church paved the way, by giving in to the synthesis mind. And the synthesis mind still seeks to cooperate in these "common" efforts.

Influence on New England Puritanism

This synthesis mind of the Cambridge Platonists helped greatly to undermine the faith of the New England Puritans. It used to be said that one of the great mysteries in religious history is the quick deterioration of New England Puritanism. More recently, however, we have begun to be aware of some of the reasons for the sudden collapse. In the course of the last couple of decades men like Samuel Morison, Perry Miller and Joseph Haroutunian *(Piety versus Moralism)* have added new comprehension to what took place.

From the beginning Puritanism was not the same as Genevan Calvinism: a strong dose of late medieval Wyclif-like content was present. (See e.g. T. C. Hall, *The Religious Background of American Culture.*) The standard authorities of the Puritans were more often than not Protestant scholastics like Keckermann and Alsted, rather than Calvin. A form of intellectualism quickly arose in New England. It was not long before men were finding their *formulations* of the doctrine more the matter of faith than the great scriptural verities themselves. There was an almost naive fascination with Reason, and the logic of Peter Ramus was their tool. Moreover, the formulations were often more after the fashion of the Cambridge Platonists than has, until very recently, been recognized. Cambridge Platonism was *prevalent* quite early. It was the source of Jonathan Edwards' idealism.

Jonathan Edwards is a controversial figure. Many Calvinists think of him as a great Calvinist. I suppose it all depends on what you mean by Calvinist. If one applies a narrowly theological criterion one will get one picture. The fact is that Edwards was influenced by the Cambridge Platonists, Malebranche and Berkeley, Locke and Newton, at least as far as the supposed world of Nature (!) is concerned. The Great Awakening (1734-35) to which he so greatly contributed was a message of redemption for the individual heart and called for individual fruits of righteousness. But of the apostate patterns of thought at work in the social-economic-political life of his time Edwards had little or nothing to say. Yet New England was rapidly becoming involved in the ways of the Old World, striving for commercial success, competing for profits, etc. The spirit of European nationalism, capitalism and rationalism, with its apparatus of political and legal theory, was everywhere taking possession of the hearts and lives of men. The influence of the synthesis made Edwards impotent to deal with this baleful drift. At the critical moment there was no *integral* Christian witness to stem the tide running towards the Enlightenment theory of the founders of the American Federal Government.

Scottish Realism and Its Effects

The second movement I want to discuss for just a moment is known as Scottish Realism, a movement which had a devastating influence upon American Presbyterian circles. The person of Jonathan Edwards provides the transition from the one to the other and the connection of New England Puritanism with Middle Atlantic Presbyterianism. In 1722 Edwards, a Yale man, had accepted a call to a Scotch Presbyterian church in New York. In 1708 the colony of Connecticut, following the opinion of Stoddard, had adopted the Saybrook Platform, by which regional associations of ministers were set up. From then on that colony so closely approximated the Presbyterian system that very cordial relations sprang up with the new Presbyterian centres of New York and New Jersey. At the end of his life again Edwards served briefly as president of the College of New Jersey, which was to become Princeton University.

Before those first years of the eighteenth century we know very little of Presbyterians in the American colonies. The Scottish Presbyterians, who had been encouraged to colonize northern Ireland a century before (the Scotch-Irish, the group to which your speaker belongs), began, under the economic and religious suppression that characterized the beginning of Queen Anne's reign, to undertake a mighty emigration to the American colonies about 1710.

The beginning of the eighteenth century was a critical time for Scotland. Since the Union with England (1707) Deism and Enlightenment ideas generally spread rapidly there. These influences were quickly felt among the Scotch-Irish in Ireland and in the American colonies.

The new century also saw a veritable "Scottish Renaissance", which placed the Scottish universities in the very forefront of European culture. Sons of the Church had a great deal to do with it. But, as in other countries, a division arose in the Church between the Evangelicals (who sympathized with the Whitefield revivals and rued the passing of the older Calvinism) and the Moderates (who, though nominally orthodox, tended to emphasize eloquent preaching, ethics, natural theology, scholarship and free philosophic inquiry.) By the middle of the century the Moderates had gained possession of the universities of Glasgow, Aberdeen and Edinburgh. At this point the "Scottish school" of philosophy emerges. Of it Sydney Ahlstrom of Yale University wrote in a recent article in the periodical *Church History* (Sept., 1955): ". . . it is more accurate to see the Scottish philosophers as a liberal vanguard, even as theological revolutionaries, than to preserve the traditional picture of genteel conservatives bringing reason to the service of a decadent orthodoxy".

The Surrender of the Reformed Faith

Jonathan Edwards, who had, you recall, come down to be president of the College of New Jersey, died in 1758. Ten years later, in 1768, John Witherspoon came to America to assume the presidency of the College. Though himself an Evangelical, he introduced Thomas Reid (1710-96) and Scottish realism as the tool by which orthodox theology could be defended against Humean scepticism, Deism and French revolutionary ideas. Yet in its views on reason, natural theology, conscience, the freedom of the will, and virtue, Scottish realism is itself a kind of practical rationalism. For that reason it quickly had taken over Harvard's new Divinity School, and had become a part of much early Unitarianism. It had also become the philosophical tool *par excellence* of the New England theology that followed upon Edwards and the Great Awakening, a movement which culminated in Nathaniel William Taylor, professor of theology in Yale Divinity School.

In the light of all that it is passing strange that it also came to be adopted by Archibald Alexander, the first professor of Princeton Theological Seminary, and by Charles Hodge, his pupil, whose textbook "Systematic Theology" I still used as a main textbook in Westminster Seminary. From Hodge the ideas of the movement permeated American Presbyterianism. Let me quote the *Church History* article of Ahlstrom once more. "Consider, for example, Alexander's 'Outlines of Moral Science', which Hodge, in lieu of any work on the subject by himself, considered to be the epitome of correct ethical reasoning. Any reader unaware that its author was one of the nation's most inflexible champions of the Old School Calvinism would assume on reading this book by itself, that is was written, perhaps, by some mild English Latitudinarian bent on mediating the views of Butler, Reid and Price. What is important here, though, is that these attitudes brought into Hodge's *Systematic Theology* what one Dutch Calvinist called "the stains of Humanism". The foundations of Hodge's ethic and his conception of natural theology are Scottish rather than Calvinistic". (The Dutch Calvinist to whom Ahlstrom refers is actually our own Dr. Danhof.) Ahlstrom goes on to point out that in the *orthodox* seminaries theology "lost its Reformation Bearings". He sees this—I think correctly—as partly attributable to the humanistic orientation of the Hutcheson-Reid tradition. To quote again: "As this philosophy was adopted, the fervent theocentricity of Calvin was sacrificed . . . Self-consciousness became the oracle of religious truth . . . The adoption of the benign and optimistic anthropology of the Scottish Moderates by American Calvinists veiled the very insights into human nature which were a chief strength of Calvin's theology. Scottish Realism accelerated the long trend toward rational theology . . . a neo-rationalism developed . . . Reformed theology was thus emptied of its most dynamic element. A kind of rationalistic *rigor mortis* set in." And to think that we have to be told this by a professor in Yale Divinity School!

To bring to an end this story about the Scottish realists I

want to quote once more from Ahlstrom. "In conclusion we may say, therefore, that the profound commitment of orthodox theology to the apologetical keeping of the Scottish philosophy made traditional doctrines so lifeless and static that a new theological turn was virtually inevitable. Certainly there is no mystery as to why end-of-century theology in America turned with such enthusiasm to evolutionary idealism, the social gospel, and the 'religion of feeling'. It was in search of the relevant and the dynamic."

William James' Comment

An interesting light on this whole sad tale of the influence of synthesis-thinking upon orthodox Christianity is shed by a remark William James made in his *Pragmatism* (1907). "Religious philosophy," he said in the first lecture of that book, "in our day and generation is, among us English-reading people, of two main types. One of these is more radical and aggressive, the other has more the air of fighting a slow retreat. By the more radical wing of religious philosophy I mean the so-called transcendental idealism of the Anglo-Hegelian school, the philosophy of such men as Green, the Cairds, Bosanquet, and Royce. This philosophy has greatly influenced the more studious members of our protestant ministry. It is pantheistic, and undoubtedly it has already blunted the edge of the traditional theism in protestantism at large. That theism remains, however. It is the lineal descendant, through one stage of concession after another, of the dogmatic scholastic theism still taught rigorously in the seminaries of the catholic church. For a long time it used to be called among us the philosophy of the Scottish school. It is what I meant by the philosophy that has the air of fighting a slow retreat. Between the encroachments of the Hegelians and other philosophers of the 'Absolute', on the one hand, and those of the scientific evolutionists and agnostics, on the other, the men that give us this kind of a philosophy, James Martineau, Professor Bowne, Professor Ladd and others, must feel themselves rather tightly squeezed. Fair-minded and candid as you like, this philosophy is not radical in temper. It is eclectic, a thing of compromise, that seeks a *modus vivendi* above all things. It accepts the facts of Darwinism, the facts of cerebral physiology, but it does nothing active or enthusiastic with them. It lacks the victorious and aggressive note. It lacks *prestige* in consequence; whereas absolutism has a certain *prestige* due to the more radical style of it."

James has caught the spirit of the synthesis-mind. "Through one stage of concession after another". In Cambridge Platonism and Scottish realism the integral POWER of the Word of God was not present to hold the hearts of men in the Truth. The heart of the synthesis-thinker is rather inclined to look to the world around him to seek a *modus vivendi*. Lacking the Truth, the synthesis-mind occupies itself with seeking "moments" of truth in the Lie. Sooner or later—lacking divine intervention—it will find itself *in the grip of the Lie*.

Rejection of All Synthesis Required

To understand Synthesis perfectly, and its consequences, just imagine what would have happened if our second representative or Office-bearing man, Jesus Christ, when, like Adam, he was tempted of Satan in the wilderness, had taken each of the devil's tempting words and looked for, even expressed a measure of agreement with, the "moments" of truth in them (without which the Lie cannot even exist since it is only a Distortion of the Truth)! That is precisely what our first parent *did*, and *fell from his place*. But the heart of the man Christ was held in the grip of the Truth, and he gave to each of Satan's tempting words the *integral answer of the Truth*. Because of what He did it is possible for the apostle to enjoin us to "stand fast in the liberty wherewith Christ has made us free and be not entangled again with the yoke of bondage" (Gal. 5:1).

I must close. I hope you appreciate better the Reformed heritage you have brought from the Netherlands. For the faithful witness of men like Groen van Prinsterer and Kuyper and the others who have followed in their line has served to lift us up out of the vast, seemingly inexorable Drift of "western Christianity" and to bring us back to the simple and charged heart of the Christian religion: *Ton serviteur, Mon Seigneur*. It is this that at first makes it difficult for all of you to find your way in your new homeland. But when you have seen the nature of God's THESIS and of the variety of human ANTITHESES there can be no hesitation as to the course we must pursue. *No Synthesis;* not even in the form of the emasculated message: Jesus saves. But a "seeing" from out of the religious Centre of how the lines of reformational activity are to be drawn throughout the length and breadth of God's creation, to bring our subjective life *integrally* into conformity with the Law of creation, the creation-ordinances. That is the Message of God's Kingdom of *Righteousness!*

Permit me to close with a Dutch citation from Prof. K. J. Popma, followed by an English translation within brackets. "De Christus maakt de Zijnen tot tweede afdeling van Zijn leger, waarvan Hij Zelf Aanvoerder en eerste afdeling is . . . . Hij gaat voort, overwinnende, *en neemt de Zijnen in die overwinning mee . . . schakelt de Zijnen in Zijn machtsvorming in.* Daarom is het altijd de moeite waard, daarom is het ons *leven* waard, Christelijke scholen te stichten, Christelijke politiek en Christelijk sociaal leven te willen nastreven, te staan naar Christelijke wetenschap en Christelijke wijsbegeerte. Dat is *alles* waard: want te delen in de machtsvorming van Christus, dat maakt al het mensenwerk glanzend en heerlijk, midden in de erbarmelijkheid van onze pogingen, in de zwakheid van onze ondernemingen en in de kortzichtigheid van ons overleg." ("Christ makes of His people a second division in His army of which He is himself the Commander and first division . . . . He goes forth, conquering, *and carries His people along with Him in His victory . . . links them to His achieving of the mastery.* Therefore it is always worth every effort, therefore it is worth our very *life,* to establish Christian schools, to strive for Christian politics and a Christian social order, to aim at Christian scientific pursuits and Christian philosophy. This is worth *everything:* for sharing in Christ's achieving of the mastery makes all human endeavors radiant and glorious amid the pitifulness of our efforts, the weakness of our undertakings and the short-sightedness of our management.)

Where each of us is ready to say, "I would be willing to *die* for that" there is reason to rejoice that the Lord has already *turned* the course of our history. *The future of Canada and of this North American continent lies in the decision of our hearts.*

Lecture IV

Scientific and Pre-Scientific*

Mr. Chairman, I want to thank you for your gracious words of introduction. Further, I wish both to express the deep satisfaction I feel at being here at this second Unionville Study Conference and, in particular, to thank the responsible authorities for the honour they bestowed upon me when for the second time they invited me to be one of your lecturers.

I must confess, Mr. Chairman, that I am still rubbing my eyes and trying to realize that Unionville days are here again. It is remarkable, the hold that this place has come to have upon us. Yet I could not say that it is strange. What took place here just one year ago has been occupying many of us in one way or another ever since. For it was no small thing, that first Unionville Conference. We who were here during those all too brief days in that beautiful beginning of September, 1959, witnessed the POWER of God at work to change the direction of student lives.

The First 'Unionville'

It was here that Christian students became aware of the fact that their being students did not in the first or deepest sense constitute them (as for purposes of statistics) a certain class in Canadian society, but is before all else to be seen as an historical unfolding of the richly varied structure of the Kingdom of God as it comes to expression in this land. That, in a word,

---

* This chapter and the following one present lectures given one year after the ones contained in the foregoing chapters.

was Unionville, 1959: a deepening realization that the calling to be a student <u>is an aspect of the dynamically developing Kingdom of God.</u> In this way we re-discovered that the *roots* of our lives are not fed in some particular civil society called Canada or the United States of America — such a view only gives rise to sickly national*isms* — but rather in that heavenly fellowship of faith, in that unity in the Truth, that is only to be found in Christ Jesus the Lord. We acquired perspective here, insight. We learned to 'place' things, to see what is root and what the branches. The Word of God opened up to us here in a new and radical way, with the result that we saw who we are and what we are doing. We saw ourselves in the deepest dimension of our lives as SERVANTS OF GOD in the Kingdom of Christ, to whom the WORD of God has been given in order that we may be perfect, thoroughly furnished unto all good works, also in our civil communities, and also in our scholarship.

Fruits of 'Unionville'

Not only the reports that have reached me of lives changed and the letters which I have received, but in general a firming up that I have been able to notice in Canada of our resolve to live, also as students, by the light of the Word of God, — these things have convinced me that Unionville was indeed a crucial turning-point, in the first place for many of us as individuals, but — and this is most important — for all of us Christian students *collectively*. Since the first Unionville Conference there has been a more conscious taking up of our collective task as Christian students. In the interval between that conference and this one at least two student organizations have been set up, one at Toronto University and another at the University of Western Ontario in London. They are young organizations, hesitant, not always sure of exactly how they must go; they need proper guidance desperately; but they are determined, because they were born of a genuine faith that the Word of God does direct our student path. This, I would propose to you, represents substantial growth in the Kingdom of God in Canada. And it would not surprise me at all if one of the early fruits of our Unionville Conferences would be an organization of students from the Maritimes to British Columbia, similar to the C.S.B. (Calvinistische Studentenbeweging) in The Netherlands, which would foster throughout the year and more systematically than we can do now, a deepened understanding of what it is to be a Christian student, what it is to study in a Christian way, what it is to build up an integrated body of scientific knowledge that is in-formed by the light of God's Word. After last year who would dare say that God will not be pleased to give us just that?

There is one more comment that I wish to make. Since Unionville-I there has been a noticeable heightening of joy in our lives. I know, because I have repeatedly observed it. Perhaps it would be better to speak of 'blessedness' rather than of 'joy'; for one may be sad or distressed and still be blessed. This too is not strange when we stop to think about what Prof. K. J. Popma has written in the first chapter of his fine book, *Eerst de Jood maar ook de Griek*. Men are called to a task *and to blessedness*. But blessedness is not a reward that follows upon the fulfiling of the task; it accompanies the doing of it. Note Ps. 1 and Ps. 119:1, 2 and the beatitudes of Christ. What we have experienced during and since our first conference is just this, that it is blessed to assume in obedience the task given. No wonder we cherish such keen expectations for this second conference. And now, here we are together again, this time with many new faces, at Mrs. Madsen's Cherry Hill Farm, at Unionville.

'Unionville' a Matter of Principle

Mr. Chairman, you will understand from what I have said why I wish to address you as I did last year, as: Young People of the Reformation in Canada. It is not blood, Dutch or otherwise, it is not a particular national background as such that brings us together here, but the Reformation faith. It is *always* ultimately *a common faith* that brings men together and establishes any genuine community. And such ultimate faiths are not a matter of geography, climate and historical development. That is why classical humanists, logical positivists, neo-thomists, and socialists can be found in all parts of the world. It is why we here, though still in large part immigrants from The Netherlands, can constitute a genuinely Canadian or American movement. But then it is extremely important, of course, that we make clear by our actions that we are not interested in the first place in extending Dutch ways of thinking and Dutch customs and institutions, and that we clearly lay the accent on our faith and our principle.

Mr. Chairman, I consider this matter to be of such fundamental importance for our young Christian immigrants that I should like, with your permission, to take just a moment more to say something further about it. Let me reiterate, it is not Dutch custom or national history as such that is our concern here in Canada, but solely *the supra-temporal Principle of our lives.*

A Timely Illustration

I think I can illustrate what I particularly have in mind by relating an incident that took place earlier this summer. With my family I was enjoying a badly needed vacation in eastern Ontario. One day at one of the nearby lakes I fell into conversation with a man who proved not only to be the head of a primary school in that vicinity but also to have occupied some position in the national government in Ottawa. We chatted in friendly fashion for a few minutes about the differences between Canadian and American high schools, but when he found that I, an American, had some kind of connection with Dutch immigrants in Canada, his attitude changed somewhat. First he asked me if it were true that the Dutch in a certain nearby community were going to open a Christian school in September. I told him that I had heard that they would. At once he showed signs of apprehension and came directly to his point: "Well," he said, "you are an American. What do you think will become of Canada if every national group that comes here proceeds to set up its own schools? Why, we'll have chaos here." He spoke with some feeling. My reply to him was, "But most of the groups that come to Canada do not do this sort of thing, do they?" And I paused for a moment for *that* to sink in. And then I went on, "Moreover, these schools are not really *Dutch* schools, even though they may seem to you at present to be that because of the natural initial language difficulties. They are not the transplanting of some kind of *national* institution. They are not even, like Lutheran and Roman Catholic schools, a sort of extension of a church denomination." I know that this is a touchy point, because in the States too in the last century we had almost as many Lutheran churches as there are northern European countries. "These schools," I told this Canadian educator, "are based on deep convictions of faith about what our human life is and how it is to be lived; they are dictated by *principle.* They are organized by Christian believers of Protestant conviction, and ideally all Canadian families who share the faith of the Protestant Reformation can participate in them."

Our Principle and the Alternatives

"But *we* give religious instruction in our schools," this educator countered. I showed that I was puzzled about how a school that is *public* can give religious instruction that would be satisfactory to a particular faith, and asked him what he understood by religious education. Then I knew that he would not be able to satisfy me. For, you know, there are only two answers that can be given to this question by the defenders of the public school. Such people understand by religious education either 1) *moralism*, i.e. the inculcating of certain moral attitudes of behaviour supposedly *common* to all the great religions of the world but considered as detached from the *religious* tenets of any one of them and valid in their own right as *moral* perceptions, or 2) instruction in the *history* of the world's great religions. The first position was held by at least one of the men who helped carve out the American democracy, viz. Thomas Jefferson. Jefferson once wrote, "We should not intermeddle with the particular dogmas in which all religions differ, and which are *totally unconnected with morality*" (italics mine). It was his position that society will best be served by observing those moral precepts in which all religions agree. "But," he wrote in his famous *Notes on the State of Virginia*, "it does me no injury for my neighbour to say there are twenty gods, or no God. It neither picks my pocket, nor breaks my leg." For Jefferson *true religion is morality*, and morality stands on its own feet. This belief is one of the deepest strata of American conviction about its public life.

But the Canadian educator with whom I was talking represented the second solution: he explained that in their schools they give lessons in the history of religion, and that they do it because they believe religious instruction to be essential and foundational for a soundly functioning democracy. In reply I said that it was not clear to me just exactly how by their telling of stories they proposed to develop that soundness of life necessary for his properly functioning democracy.

The Word of God our Principle

And that, my young friends, is the whole issue between the defenders of the public schools and us. With respect to the one argument there is no morality that is not rooted in the Divine

Imperative; with respect to the second, stories, even though they be stories about religion, do not bolster sagging democracies, — or empires either, for that matter. To be whole-heartedly committed to a belief is very different from observing that same belief from the outside. What is needed for the direction of life is *faith,* a hearty acceptance of, a binding commitment to the Word that God has given to be the Guide or Norm or Principle of our life. For that Word is after all simply God Himself directing Himself graciously to us, addressing us in His peculiarly sovereign Power. His Word is a power that begets to new life (I Pet. 1:23. This passage with surrounding verses also refutes Jefferson's position about the relation between religion and morality); the divine Word is that Arché the Greek philosophers were forever seeking after, the starting-point of our (new) life that at the same time governs, directs its future course, in short, our *Principle.*

Our Debate with Our Times

The conversation that I have been relating to you came to an end at this point, but later I got to thinking it all over. In one sense I could very well understand the anxiety of this man. If our neighbours should get from us the idea that we are struggling to erect Christian schools, Christian labour organizations and Christian political parties just because it is an old Dutch custom, then their irritation and, where they see our work as a threat to national integration or as positively divisive, their open hostility could easily be understood, perhaps in a sense even justified. And that is how this man was looking at us. Yet for us to give such an impression would be a betrayal of our highest calling. Our debate with our times is no less than a debate about *principle*. This word may not be popular or understood in our day, but what it refers to is real. Let us simply recall the Latin word *principium,* meaning 'beginning', 'commencement', 'origin'. The debate of our times in which we must all mingle is a debate about the ultimate faith that, whether recognized as such or not, directs our goings by taking possession of the 'beginnings' of our lives (our hearts).

Principle, the Question of Our Time

As a result of the conversation we had had I felt that the man had been relieved of at least some of his anxiety about a divided Canada, but, particularly important, that the debate had irrevocably been shifted to where it properly belongs. Principle is something still somewhat respected in western society as that ultimate loyalty of men which the state may not touch. It will have to remain that way if we are to be distinguished from totalitarian thinkers. It will have to remain that way even though the fact is inescapable that men are deeply divided on this matter of ultimate faith. There are only two ways to do away with this ultimate dividedness of the human race. One is to attempt to create a common faith by conviction or hidden pressure. This effort has been made on a grand scale in our modern centuries following upon the Wars of Religion, and it appears to be a thorough-going failure. The other way is by a frank surrender of our cherished democratic freedom. Everywhere today human society is fundamentally disturbed by the conflicting principles which men accept for their lives. I believe it is the basic question of human life, one which only the living and powerful Word of God can elucidate.

The Seriousness of the Situation

In this critical situation, Mr. Chairman, the fact that I return again this year in my lectures to a consideration of the basic *principle* of the Christian's life should require no apology. Nothing else urges itself more constantly upon our attention than this. A Cornell University sociologist reported this year that American college students are "politically disinterested and apathetic". Her explanation was significant: they are apathetic, she said, because "there are no clearly defined programs around which to rally, no clearly defined answers to the problems which their generation confronts". She might have said that both they and their times lack an acknowledged guiding principle. Our theatre has no vitality because it lacks any conviction about the nature of man and his life. Indeed, our whole western society seems to be drifting without any sense of direction, not only in the foreign policies of the several nations, but in all its aspects. Bertrand Russell has written somewhere that the dogmatic systems and norms of behaviour no longer have the hold on men they once had, that men are often in real doubt as to what is good and bad and even ask themselves whether good and evil are anything more than old superstition, and that if they try to solve such problems, these appear to be too difficult for them. His sobering summary conclusion is that men cannot discover a single clear aim to be striven after or a single clear principle that could lead them. Evidently, if we Christians are to make a clear and relevant witness in the second half of the twentieth century we shall have to be clear about this matter of principle.

This Year's Lectures

The lectures that I propose to deliver to you in this conference, Mr. Chairman, presuppose, in a way, my lectures of last year, now available in the paperback *Christian Perspectives, 1960*.[1] Yet I trust they will be sufficiently understood even by those of you who are not yet acquainted with the work we did here at that time. The lecture for this morning is entitled SCIENTIFIC AND PRE-SCIENTIFIC. In my second lecture I propose to talk about SPHERE-SOVEREIGNTY.

Mr. Chairman, I shall now proceed to enter upon the discussion of our first topic. Though the title SCIENTIFIC AND PRE-SCIENTIFIC may seem somewhat prosaic, I must say that I can scarcely imagine a subject which it would be more important to discuss with Christian students than the one we now have before us, especially when the Christian students in question are compelled, as many of you here are, to attend one of our modern secular universities.

Importance of Our First Subject

From my observation of Christian students over a period now of slightly more than twenty-five years I am convinced that almost without exception the student is lost to *integral* Christianity not somewhere down the years of his university experiences, but at the very outset. Susanne K. Langer is right when she says in her book, *Philosophy in a New Key,* that the way in which a philosophical movement *formulates* its problems is more significant than the solutions it subsequently arrives at. "Its answers," she writes, "establish an edifice of facts; but its questions make the frame in which its picture of facts is plotted. They make more than the frame; they give the angle of perspective, the palette, the style in which the picture is drawn — everything except the subject. In our questions lie our *principles of analysis,* and our answers may express whatever those principles are able to yield." (p. 1 f.) So it is also, I am convinced, with the unsuspecting Christian student who enters one of our universities. For the

---
[1] In this edition contained in chapters I-III.

university at its very portals formulates, as it were, for the incoming student the problem of life.

The innocent freshman does not realize that the very *existence* of the university involves the philosophical problem as to its *place*, as to the *place* of science *(die Wissenschaft)* in the whole of life. He is, as a matter of fact, caught unawares at a very weak moment in his life. His coming to the university marks a transition to a new period of his life: he becomes more independent and in his enlarged freedom looks to the world of science as somehow *his* mature life. He is fired with a zeal to master some one or more branches of scientific knowledge. He is open to the influences of the scientific mind. At this critical juncture only at his peril will our fledgling look upon the university as merely a collection of *scholars* engaged in what to him appears to be the very high calling of scientific pursuits or even, as he will soon hear it called, the pursuit of truth, and overlook thereby the fact that the university is also a concentrated microcosm of the modern mind. For the university is also and inevitably an association of *men,* and in spite of so much modern theory, men are more than scientific minds: they are *believers.* The men who staff our modern universities largely share in the faith of the modern world.

Scientism is Faith in Science

In order to explain the predicament of our hypothetical freshman I must right here say something briefly about that faith. The modern age has been described as the age of science, and also as the age of revolution. If you will permit me, I will at once substitute in the first description the word 'scientism' for 'science' because I think that it more exactly expresses the sense of what has largely taken place in our modern centuries. Only the further development of my lecture can justify this substitution. And if on some future occasion I may have the pleasure of addressing you again I shall try to show you that there is also an intimate connection between scientism and revolution.[1] At the present moment, however, I am interested only in the former of the two characterizations of our age. Just a word about it.

The word 'scientism' is one of those 'ism' words we talked about last year.[2] The 'ism' suggests that an exaggerated emphasis

---

[1] This promise was partially fulfilled when I discussed "Scriptural Religion and Political Task" in my Unionville Lectures for 1961. These lectures are published in the (brown) *Christian Perspectives, 1962,* esp. p. 198 ff.
[2] See above, p. 47 f.

has been put upon something in our theoretical explanation of that thing. Thus the word 'scientism' suggests that in our modern theory too great a role has been assigned to 'scientia', a role, that is, greater than it has been given to play in the world by reason of the divine ordinances. The word 'scientia' itself is a Latin equivalent for our English 'knowledge'. We find it, for example, at the beginning of the second chapter of the first book of Thomas a Kempis' *Imitatio Christi:* "*Omnis homo naturaliter scire desiderat, sed scientia sine timore Dei quid importat?*" Important to notice is the use of 'scientia' for 'knowledge' where the writer is warning his readers against the dangers of intellectualism in religion. This Thomas no doubt had Thomas Aquinas in mind, and the whole ensuing tribe of scholastic philosophers; for the first part of the sentence I quoted is, as you will perhaps have recognized, a literal translation of the first sentence of Aristotle's *Metaphysics*. In his excellent little book *Humanism and Theology* (p. 14) Werner Jaeger writes about this passage, "When Thomas a Kempis repeats these words and adds: 'But what is the good of human wisdom without the fear of God?' he obviously intends to hit the pride of the scholastic philosophers of his time and their heated controversies about dogmatic questions which they carried on in their classrooms with the methods of Aristotelian dialectic." Thus 'scientia' here conveys a scientifically discursive kind of knowledge which Thomas a Kempis contrasts (*Imit. Chr.* ch. 3 sect. 2) with the knowledge that comes from hearing the eternal Word speak to us. I think it is significant, by way of contrast, that when Calvin speaks about the knowledge of God at the beginning of his *Institutio,* he does not use this word 'scientia' but that other Latin word for knowledge, 'cognitio'. The latter word appears to have been free of undesirable connotations.

From what has now been said you will have gathered that the word 'scientism' means a theoretical view that exaggerates the place that science and scientific knowledge actually have in life. It is in this sense that we shall be using the word in the sequel. You can see at once that scientism, as a "view that exaggerates" is not the same as science. It is rather a conviction-of-faith about science, and a wrong one (exaggeration) at that. Science, the scientific method, does not, *can* not give rise to scientism. The latter, as I hope to show, is a philosophical viewpoint like idealism or materialism; it is a view about the *place* of science in the whole of our life. Basically, scientism is modern man's worship, the expression of his apostate religion. Here and there, and especially among more recent irrationalistic thinkers, there has been a recognition of the limited sphere of scientific knowledge (as e.g. in Karl Jaspers' reply to Rudolf Bultmann, cf. the Noonday paperback, *Myth and Christianity*, p. 6).

Illustrations of Scientistic Attitude

What *concretely* is meant by scientism? Let me give a couple of preliminary examples. In the modern world generally the criterion of everything that is good and worthy of our attention has been whether it is 'scientific'. The modern world is convinced that science holds the last word. For John Dewey and many others there must come in the 20th century a reconstruction of philosophy because previous attempts at philosophizing had all been 'pre-scientific'. (Positivism and logical positivism, the philosophical movements that in recent decades have all but dominated the universities on our continent, have tried desperately to make philosophy 'scientific'.) Rudolf Bultmann's now widely discussed method of 'Entmythologisierung' (de-mythologizing) would remove from the biblical writings all traces of their primitive, 'pre-scientific' world-picture, in order to allow the divine revelation itself to meet the 'scientific' test. (Scientific knowledge, i.e. knowledge gained by scientific methods and thus meeting the test of those methods, has been acclaimed in great areas of our modern world as the only proper and adequate avenue to the truth. Today war must be 'scientific', we must have 'scientific' breakfasts, 'scientific' toothbrushes, 'scientific' sex education for the schools, 'scientific' lovemaking for our young couples and a 'scientific' way of planning our families and rearing our children. We even have 'scientific' socialists. Both the Nazis and the Marxists appealed to science for their opposite views of human nature. But also our American former ambassador Joseph E. Davies interpreted his laissez-faire conception of human nature in biological terms. In Great Britain the official pacifist movement published a pamphlet entitled, *Is Pacifism Scientific or Sentimental?*, the conclusion of which was that pacifism and not militarism receives scientific sanction and is therefore to be approved by *modern* man. In the May 5, 1958 issue of *Time* (p. 36) the famous physicist J. Robert Oppenheimer is reported to have told the *Paris-Presse:* "I believe that only a world council of wise men can assure peace on a scientific basis. Throughout the world, scientists are ready and eager to co-operate in such a project. I believe that we can and will eventually cure atomic terror just as doctors have succeeded in combatting malaria — by banding together." And so we could go on. Why, it has got so bad that we are almost afraid to ask our neighbour whether he saw the beautiful sunset, because he might just be a scientist and look disdainfully down upon us in our primitive world from out of his superior knowledge that, scientifically speaking — for him the equivalent of truthfully speaking —, there is no sunset.

Scientism's Strange Reversal of Things

If in all this all that was meant was that scientific research can contribute something to enrich our knowledge of these things, we could and would have no objection. Science is an important gift of God to man. But that what is meant goes far deeper can perhaps be felt from our last remark about the sunset. Science is here not something to enrich a knowledge we already have; science is everything, at least, everything that is respectable. *Normal experiences of life must be broken down and re-formed according to the demands of the scientific point of view.* As we saw in the examples given, 'pre-scientific' was used with the sense 'before the advent of the scientific method, which has now in these last days opened up to us the possibility of arriving at truth'. That is to say, 'pre-scientific' is here equivalent to 'unscientific', 'worthless'. What is 'pre-scientific' cannot be related to the truth.

We have here that reversal of things that is the strange heart of scientism. Life and experience, which always precede science, are second; science, which always must be second, is first. Descartes, who is generally taken as the one who introduced the modern manner of philosophizing, is the best example of what I mean. His method consists in having the scientific (geometrical) reason call all previous experience (i.e. experience previous to the application of the scientific method) into question until that scientific reason itself should discover some scientifically ascertainable absolute starting-point for experience. From this scientifically fixed starting-point the reason (scientific, of course) proceeds to build up, in that supposedly scientific way Descartes, Spinoza and others called *more geometrico,* a new experience that would meet the scientific test. This latter experience, then, because it supposedly meets the scientific test, is the genuine experience. Here is the world and the word of truth. This is what we mean by scientism's reversal of the natural order. It replaces the experience of a lifetime and the practical wisdom of the ages; it is a substitute for religion. In his preface to Karl Mannheim's *Ideology and Utopia,* Prof. Louis Wirth, a prominent sociologist, writes: ". . . the voice of science is heard with a respect approximating the sanctity which formerly was accorded only to authoritarian, religious pronouncements." His words show that scientism is not science but the way we *hear* science, our religious giving of our hearts to science.

A Critical Situation for the Christian Student

This scientism is still essentially the faith of the men comprising the teaching staffs of our modern universities. In some individuals that faith appears in a more militant and virulent form; in others it is more a placid, unquestioned basic motor force covertly operative in the way their lives are lived. In the university, as in the modern world, this standpoint of modern faith is not so much argued as presupposed. It may also be argued somewhere along the line, but that is not the most dangerous moment in the student's life. For by the time the question comes to be *argued* the student's *heart* has already been claimed. *All he now does is to accept the argued position as "self-evident."*

What can our incoming freshman of a moment ago possibly be expected to know of all these long-standing issues, so momentous for the outcome of his life? Practically nothing. He simply is not aware that the university is a concentrated cross-section of the modern world, and that it will not only teach him the science he so eagerly covets just at this period of his life, but will also feed him large doses of a *view of life* which sees the pursuit of scientific knowledge as *the* human ideal, leading to human blessedness.

A Personal Illustration of This

Perhaps I can heighten the vividness of the impression I am trying to create by telling you something of my own experience as a very immature student at the University of Pennsylvania a quarter of a century ago. In the fall of the year I entered a course in the history of modern philosophy, and our professor, a brilliant logician, began at once to discuss Descartes with us and his method of radical doubt that I have already referred to. Today we would say that this method of teaching was 'existential': he used our class as an illustration of Descartes' meaning. "Right in this class," he said to us, "conflicting dogmatic beliefs of traditional religious groups are represented: orthodox and liberal Judaism, Roman Catholicism, orthodox and liberal Protestantism, humanism, atheism. Now, how are we who represent these faiths going to talk with each other? When we begin to argue with each other we find that our traditional beliefs are not so clearly evident to us as we had hitherto supposed. Moreover, on what *common basis* can we discuss the "truth" of our several faiths unless we are all willing to abandon for the moment the dogmatic starting-points of our several religious commitments and to find another starting-point that is *universally acceptable* to the scientific reason?" At the end of the period as we were already leaving the room the professor dared us to free ourselves of our past and make a new beginning on a rational basis that would be acceptable to all reasonable persons.

What would you have done? I was a serious student; I wanted more than anything else at that moment to enter into the beckoning mysteries of the history of modern philosophy. Well, I remember vividly that as I was walking home that noon I happened to pass through a small city park. I stopped and stood by a tree in the center of the park completely absorbed in my sober thoughts. I took out my pocket-knife and began to carve my initials in the bark of the tree, while deep within me I was saying to myself, Should I or should I not; dare I or don't I dare? That was to say, Should I throw overboard the faith in which I had been reared — probably it would only be for a moment, anyhow — and begin again, in the scientific manner of my professor? Wasn't that, after all, the only thoroughly honest way? If my religion was true it certainly would stand the test of a scientific method. Or would it?

I did not follow the advice of my professor, but I almost did, humanly speaking. Yet I must say this here: I did not know what was going on, and for years I was unable to say why it was not right to take the professor's 'reasonable' dare. I know many Christians who took similar advice, usually with the most disastrous consequences.

Permit me one more brief illustration. Many years later when I was doing graduate work in a research society at Harvard University it happened at a dinner [Heidegger?] that a professor suddenly looked up laughing into my face and asked if I could still believe that Jesus had gone 'up' to heaven. He meant, of course, that with the modern scientific picture of the world that had arisen out of the work of Copernicus, Bruno, Kepler, Galileo, and others 'up' could be anywhere and thus nowhere in particular. By this time I was more mature and knew something about what was going on. But the disdainful attitude still hurt; it was as if you were being cut off from any body of scholars that might be expected to do useful work.

The Heart of Our Weakness

Every year, I am sure, a very large number of young students of Christian background succumb to the apparent attractions and alleged advantages of this aggressive scientism simply because they are not sufficiently believing and therefore not properly critical. It is certainly the duty of pastors to make this general situation clear to those of their young people who go to the university. To learn scientific pursuits is one thing; to adopt a scien*tistic* outlook is quite another thing: *it is, in fact, to accept an alternative to Christianity*. For scientism is a belief about the principle of our life, which it finds in the clarity and apparent secure cogency of theoretical or scientific thought. On the other hand, the Bible as the Word of God declares that *it* is that principle, and I showed in my 1959 lectures *(Christian Perspectives, 1960)* how this is in general to be understood. Obviously, the victory of scientism is the defeat of Christianity, and *vice versa*. Where students of Christian background year in year out naively accept the formulation which the modern university, mirroring the modern age, gives to the problem as to the principle of our life, the forces of the modern mind need not fear regular attendance at the churches. It is fully aware that it will receive the fattened calf in the very first year of the university. Present-day polls, for example, show a great majority of 'Christian' people, who nevertheless think of Christianity in the relativistic, evolutionistic way.

I have said that these young people are not properly critical because they are not sufficiently believing. We might do well to ponder this remark. I shall not elaborate further upon it here.

Weakness Born of Accommodation

The effectiveness of the Body of Christ in the world is greatly weakened by that other group of Christian students who in the struggle hold on somehow to a reduced religion of personal salvation but give in to the scientistic spirit in the broader reaches of life. I wish particularly to signal this grave danger; therefore I will be very concrete. I am thinking of a man who teaches in the natural sciences division of one of our larger American universities. He was raised in a genuinely Christian home and was graduated from one of our Christian colleges in the States. Today this man is very active in the organizing of student prayer meetings and in otherwise strengthening the personal faith of Christian students at his university. At the same time, he gladly associates himself with the view which sees science as limited to mathematically measured or measurable "facts" and particularly as divorced from any philosophical and religious roots and constructions. Never would you be able to get this man to admit in so many words that a great part of our activity in the creation is divorced from the fall of man and from Christ and His redemption. Nevertheless, practically and without any theoretical reflection about its possibility he accepts the modern view of the *autonomy of scientific thought*. Even here already there is open conflict in his life. But this man even believes that this modern view of the scientific enterprise is desirable because it makes possible some areas of human *community* in a world otherwise hopelessly divided. And here is that faith that science will redeem the world by breaking down boundaries of superstition and gradually setting up a human community in the truth, a faith that conflicts with what Scripture reveals about how Christ will establish His Kingdom of Truth. Hesitantly, because here he begins to feel that his ideas are getting out of hand, this man accepts the belief that as science goes on to conquer more and more of life's areas and bring its enlightenment, the sphere of human community will progressively be enlarged. Is this man a Christian or not? Of course, he is. Yet something blocks the working-out of his faith, and for all practical purposes he is a modern scientistic thinker. He has really gone over to positivism. The only thing that distinguishes him is that he sets up *limits* for his positivism: he holds that there is *also* an area of religion. *Whole-hearted* service of Christ this man cannot know; for he thinks of 'heart' pietistically, as the seat of the affective life *over against* the life of reason, and thus misses any integral conception of existence. In short, integral, biblical Christianity has departed his life. But his positivism too, like every religious faith, will go on making increasing claims upon his heart. This man is truly a house divided against itself. And for that reason the *power* of the Word of God to renew all of life from out of the heart and to bring all things into subjection to the Christ of God simply cannot operate through him as it ought. Moreover, his positivism *will effectively keep him from understanding the revelation of God aright.* His life cannot be one of increasing sanctification. And in great areas of his life there will be no blessedness. Very often in life the more positivistic a Christian becomes, the more he tries to right everything with prayer meetings. But what he needs is faith, and faith is obedience.

The Urgent Need of a Christian University

Why have I spoken at such length about one man? Because I know that to a greater or less degree he is a picture of most Christian university-trained young people who continue to show a scientific interest. This is right serious business. That is why I said at the very outset this morning that I could scarcely imagine a subject more important to discuss with Christian students than the one we have this morning. Let me say further that I can hardly imagine a better example of the need for an integrally Christian centre of scholarly research and instruction on this North American continent. For our subject involves every one of the special sciences as well as philosophy, and above all a knowledge of God's revelation in Christ. Only a university community of scholars who are all alike committed to the integral or scriptural conception of Christianity and who are abreast of their times in a number of branches of scholarship can do the job that must be done to save our young people from what is daily taking place. Let us pray for such a university; let us support the labours of the ARSS. We need leaders who 'see', and we need them *now*. There is no time to lose.

The Issue: the Relation between 'Scientific' and 'Pre-scientific'

This morning, of course, we cannot do everything. But I do wish to direct your attention in the remainder of the lecture more particularly to the relation that exists between what we have been calling 'scientific' and 'pre-scientific'.

(We have been getting acquainted with the view that scientism takes of this relationship. It says that only what has been subjected to and re-formed by the scientific method is true and sure and good. And of course the corollary of this is that what is not thus scientific is primitive or immature, false and unworthy, material for the scientific mind to re-make to truth.)

That is what was behind my reference to the sunset. The scien*tistic* thinker (not, be it noted, the scientific thinker!) has identified all proper knowledge with scientific knowledge, in particular with the mathematical methods of physics or with other areas of science that attempt to apply its methods. When we look at the earth and the sun and their mutual relations *in this particular manner,* then there is no place for a sunset. The scientistic thinker characteristically concludes that the concept 'sunset' belongs to a primitive pre-scientific generation and straightway excludes it from the body of true and valid knowledge.

The same sort of thing was involved in the Harvard professor's laughing remark to me about the ascension of Christ. From the point of view of our present scientific conception of the motions of physical bodies in space it is not possible to conceive of any absolute 'up'; such a concept the scientistic thinker would describe as 'medieval' and 'obscurantist'.

Confusion born of a Medieval Accommodation (Synthesis)

We need to take a slightly closer look at what is involved here. What the medieval men had done was to accommodate scriptural revelation to an old Greek science. These men were fully familiar with the biblical account of the earth in the book of *Genesis* as the place of God's covenantal and redemptive dealings with man, and with the second chapter of Genesis in particular, which reveals God's unusual concern for his creature, man. From that chapter they sensed that God had placed man in the centre of the creation, and from that they sensed further that the earth is the great stage of the divine-human encounter. So far these medieval men were correct. But then they went on to read this biblical revelation in the light of ancient Greek views (Aristotle and Ptolemy) about the 'physical world'. The result was that the earth was now conceived as the center of the world, a fixed center *in the physical-scientific sense.* Underneath it — in that same physical sense —

lay hell, the fumes of which could sometimes be seen rising from crevices and fissures in the earth's floor. And above the earth were the several (seven of them) spheres in which the seven known planets (including the sun) revolved. Above the last of these spheres came the incorruptible firmament (no. 8), the outer limit of the physical world, not having the motion of the spheres. From this incorruptible firmament the fixed stars were thought to be suspended like lamps. Beyond this supposed limit of the physical world the mind's eye of medieval man discerned the Ninth Heaven, to which the saints were rapt, the Primum Mobile or Crystalline sphere. At the very top of the picture there was the Empyrean or Paradise, the dwelling of the blessed and the throne of God.

This composite medieval world-picture illustrates what we mean when we say that in the medieval thought-world scriptural revelation and Greek science were accommodated to each other. This is the synthesis mind that I talked about in my last lecture last year. Medieval Christians read the Greek scientific meaning back into revelation, so that the 'up' of Jesus' ascension became confused with the 'up' of the Ptolemaic world-picture. But science, a human activity, has a history. And when subsequently the Ptolemaic picture was cast aside by men like Bruno and Copernicus, the effect upon the Church and upon the attitude of men towards the Word of God was disastrous. Not because science had disproved the scriptures, but because the medieval church had accommodated the supra-temporal Word of God to a time-conditioned scientific piece of work, understanding the former in the light of the latter, thus reversing the natural order. The science in the synthesis was indeed primitive. But there is no reason, if one does not fall into the original error, for transferring this label to the divine revelation. As religious revelation it comes first, and if it had been heartily believed medieval men might have come to see that the Ptolemaic 'world'-picture is not the *world* of scripture. ('World' is one abstracted aspect of world; world can only be understood as the covenantal fellowship of God and man in Christ-Adam.) But they did *not* see that, and the modern falling away from the Word of God and from the Church can in a very significant degree be ascribed to their 'accommodating' error.

Let me with an apt quotation from Anatole France's book *Garden of Epicurus* attempt to convey to you something of the radical change-over of mind that took place as a result, in which you can feel something of the struggle of heart, the pain, a tinge of the bitterness but also the spirit of adventure of a man forsaken of God and deprived of his heavenly Father's provision and comfort and believing himself to be on his lonely own, all features so highly characteristic of early modern man.

"In those days God had no other children than man, and all his creation was ordered in a fashion at once childlike and poetic like an immense cathedral." (But now) "we are done with the spheres and the planets under which one was born lucky or unlucky, jovial or saturnine. The solid vault of the firmament is shattered. Our eye and our thought plunge into infinite abysses of heaven. Beyond the planets we discover no longer the Empyrean of the elect and of the angels, but a hundred millions of rolling suns escorted by their cortege of obscure satellites invisible to us. In the midst of this infinity of worlds our own Sun is but a bubble of gas and our Earth but a fleck of mud."

You get the feel of a youth cast out of his parental home who, with one eye longingly fixed on the past, sets to walking bitterly towards his future, accompanying himself in his loneliness by whistling a dare-devil tune. As one man has put it somewhat sacrilegiously of Giordano Bruno, "There came the day in Bruno's life when he stepped out of his Father's House to make his way "ins Freie hinaus".

We Should Learn Our Lesson

This very important incident at the beginning of the modern age ought to teach us what grave perils are hidden in any attempt at turning the revelation of God into any specific scientific statements, — what in German we might call *"Um*deutung".

I suppose that all this was in the mind of that Harvard professor that day. But, as I have already told you, there was no opportunity on that occasion to explain to him how I thought about the matter. Actually, however, his observation had no more bearing on my thought than that other half-rhetorical question once put to me by one of Harvard's most distinguished professors: "How can you believe in God in these days when space has become so vast; where do you put Him?" For all the scriptures say about the ascension is that Jesus led the disciples to a place over against Bethany and that while they looked on he was taken up, and a cloud received him out of their sight. It ought to be clear that the 'up' here simply refers to the very ordinary, everyday experience of those disciples who remained standing on the earth, the place appointed by God to be man's home.

As we progress in our treatment of our theme I hope that there will gradually arise in you an insight into the fatal original error of scientism. That error, to put it briefly, was to take such a word as 'up' and insist that the only "true" meaning it could have was the scientific meaning that refers abstractly to relations of physical motion. In logical terms, such words were thought of as being 'univocal', i.e. as having one and only one meaning. That is why men like Rudolf Bultmann, when they read in the scriptures the words "Thou shalt not make unto thee any graven image, or any likeness of any thing that is in heaven above, or that is in the earth beneath, or that is in the water under the earth" think at once of a primitive Babylonian world-picture.

Rise of Modern Scientism: the World(!) of Matter

To carry this analysis a step closer to what I hope will be clarity let me say something of how the error of scientism arose in modern times. The modern world of thought began with a new physics and out of that physics there developed the new or modern philosophy. The philosophers of the new age considered their central task to be the achievement of a new synthesis of thought, this time in terms of the kind of reality that scientific method disclosed. We must not forget that by and large these men, though often maintaining a proper external connection with the Church, were really in their hearts men who had left behind them any genuine belief in divine revelation. They now had to fill in that empty place in their lives with something else. Their ideal was still a system of revelation, though they had abandoned the only revelation there is. They found knowledge, even valid knowledge, but only later did it dawn on them that the knowledge they could find in this way is a different sort of knowledge from what they thought they were finding. At first they agreed that *reality* was what this new science of physics told us about; for they assumed that the new physics revealed the Truth (not a truth, but the complete, final and only real Truth) about the *world,* about reality. And what

appearance / reality

was the reality that this physics disclosed? It was something called 'matter'. Matter was the name given to what the physicists held that they were measuring. And so the view arose that the "world of matter" which the physicists studied was the *real world*, the true, full and final sense of the word 'world'. Over against this was that other world of ordinary experience, — the world of concrete persons and things, events and institutions we daily come in contact with. This latter world now came to be regarded as the world of *appearance*, as opposed to the scientists' world of *reality*. The world of appearance was thus the "pre-scientific" way of viewing the world; since 'logical' came to stand for the methods of the scientists, the pre-scientific world was also the "pre-logical" world, the world as the "pre-logical" mind viewed it, a primitive, undeveloped and therefore unworthy and false representation of things. You can read this very kind of argument in the first pages of Bertrand Russell's book, *The Problems of Philosophy*.

Scientistic Attitude of Enlightenment 'Historians'

The very same pattern of thought can be found among the historians of the Age of Enlightenment, who thought of their own generation as the first to apply the scientific test to everything, and who therefore thought of all previous history as 'pre-scientific' history and for that reason not worthy of the scientific historian. They generally looked upon the past as a history of human vanities or errors. Prof. R. G. Collingwood, in his book *The Idea of History*, commenting on the fact that the interest of these historians of the early eighteenth century was restricted essentially to the modern period, has this to say (p. 78): "The real cause of this restriction of interest to the modern period was that with their narrow conception of reason they had no sympathy for, and therefore no insight into, what from their point of view were non-rational periods of human history; they only began to be interested in history at the point where it began to be the history of a modern spirit akin to their own, a scientific spirit...." Again on p. 80 Collingwood writes: "The central point of history, for these writers, is the sunrise of the modern scientific spirit. Before that, everything was superstition and darkness, error and imposture. And of these things there can be no history, not only because they are unworthy of historical study, but because there is in them no rational or necessary development: the story of them is a tale, told by an idiot, full of sound and fury, signifying nothing."

Evil Fruit of Scientism

You can see that the scientistic frame of mind leads to a misjudging, actually to a *disqualifying* of everyday experience. This was to have serious consequences for human life and society. It led, particularly in Germany, the land of *Wissenschaft par excellence,* but also in the West generally, to the phenomenon we know as the withdrawal of the scholars from the concerns of everyday life. These pursuers of 'truth for truth's sake' interested themselves in the phenomena of life only after these phenomena had been worked into the straightjacket of a theoretical construction. They lived out their lives in their studies and laboratories. In his book *The University and the Modern World* Arnold S. Nash tells us that in Germany this attitude goes back to Goethe at least, who, speaking of the indifference of his circle to the French Revolution, said, "We took no notice of news or newspapers; our object was to know Man; as for men we left them to do as they chose". Goethe was also the man who said, "Let us leave politics to diplomats and soldiers". On the very day that Hitler became the German Chancellor the wife of one of the great German professors of the day spoke of him as "The man in the cheap newspapers".

But Hitler himself understood the situation; for he wrote in *Mein Kampf* as follows: "God knows the Germans have never been lacking in 'knowledge'. Germany's trouble has been, not that the brains governing her were too little educated but too fully. The heads of the rulers were stuffed with information and empty of instinct, utterly bereft of energy and audacity . . . . Why? Because the so-called intellectual class shut itself away from the rest of the workaday world. They had no living ties with the classes below them."

The 'Absent-minded' Professor

The fact was that these German intellectuals of the pre-Hitler regime who had refused to soil their hands by engaging in politics could not recognize — still less comprehend — their fate when it stared them in the face, and they were helpless before it. I had personal experience of this fact which I shall never forget. During my time at Harvard I studied with a German scholar of world-renown. One day he told me about his last days in Berlin. He and his colleagues had been men of *Wissenschaft* in the German tradition. They came to their offices early in the morning and left late in the evening. They carried their scientific work with them in the streets and to their homes, and often wrestled with their problems in the middle of the night. But there came a sudden and rude awakening. Early one morning, this professor told me, a colleague of his had knocked on his office-door. After a whispered word they both had gone down into the street and walked along the river Spree. There the colleague had pointed to a human torso that was floating in the river. Utterly shaken, these two men had proceeded to connect this ghastly experience with rumours that had recently begun to pass around among the professors. It was the first break-through into the minds of these men of the meaning of the mortal storm that was shaking Hitler's Third Reich. When my professor told me the story it was already more than five years later, but I could still read something of incredulity in his face. This whole generation of scholars had had to be shocked into the awareness that life is more than science, and that this 'more' is so very real that it will even determine the nature of the scientific work that is to be performed. Now there was nothing left for this professor (and many others like him) to do but to flee for his personal saftey, to run away from the people and the society which by its daily toil had made his scholarly work possible, and to leave them to their ghoulish and fiery fates.

Although there has been since World War II something of a change for the better in some quarters, the scientistic withdrawal into the world of "scientific truth", the pursuit of "truth for its own sake", continues unabated. There is a good reason for that. The 'scientific mind' is not a man. With the decline of the Christian religion and the dominance of scientism for centuries, many men have to all intents and purposes reduced their lives to that thing we call the 'scientific mind'. Because of the nature of scientific thinking the attitudes and results connected with it cannot be applied easily and directly to life. Therefore such a 'reduced' modern man often can not get to feel at home in the everyday world of men and events. The easiest way is to retreat into the study or laboratory, and that is what frequently happens. Therefore, the scientistic mind is still to be found everywhere in the world. There is no hope for a change except the Truth of the Word of God make men again to be full men, men of God, perfect, thoroughly furnished unto every good work; except the fulness of life promised by Christ come to our contemporaries. Science cannot do that. Nor can a limited conception of the validity of science do it.

Varieties of the Scientistic Mind

I think it will be useful, before we proceed to the final analysis of the error of scientism, to offer you a small number of examples of the scientistic mind and its error, so destructive of life, outside the realm of physics. For while the substitution of scientific abstraction for fulness of life began in the modern world with physics, the phenomenon is not restricted to any particular area of the scientific enterprise. Let me give one example each from the fields of law, logic and theology. I have chosen them from life close by, so that they will be readily grasped.

Scientism in Law

First, an example from the field of law. Perhaps some of you here also read in a recent issue of *De Spiegel* the article entitled "De Schande van Soesterberg". There had been a head-on collision between a heavy trailer-truck and an automobile. The result: two places of business along the highway suddenly in complete ruins. This unfortunate event took place on the 28th of April, 1956. When the article appeared in the issue of June 4, 1960 there had not been any disposition of the case and none of the innocent third parties, who were now actually in need, had been paid a cent.

What was the reason for the delay? A 'nice' question, as a lawyer might say, using the word 'nice' in its nice or precise sense. It was not clear whether the chauffeur of the automobile had died of a heart attack *before* the collision, thus *causing* it, or afterwards as a *result* of it. Four years later, when some outside persons began to take an interest in the case and approached the lawyers to find out whether something could not be done to help, the lawyers, supposedly representing their clients, who were the real dupes of the affair, brought their hands together finger-tip to finger-tip and smiled blandly, but only said, "In law this is perfectly normal; Dutch law permits this sort of thing." Here is what I would call the scientific mind in practice. The legal configurations (abstractions) in this story of human misery had such a complete hold on them that life itself was excluded from the chambers of their hearts (or do such people only have heads)? The *Spiegel* reporter, thus giving unwelcome publicity to the case, concluded his article with the remark, "Perhaps the lawyers will be brought to see it as more than just an interesting legal case. More important interests are involved here." There is, of course, nothing wrong with one's spending one's life in the study of legal states of affairs, provided one is first of all a *man,* who understands the *abstract nature of scientific figures,* and the status of science as *servant of life.* But the scien*tistic* thinker does not have that understanding.

Scientism in Logic

My second example is from the area of logic. There are those who tend to treat the Word of God as though it is nothing but a series of (logical) propositions or of lingual statements. We must at once agree that in the Scriptures as they present themselves to us in our temporal existence we can find a series of logical propositions. But the question is whether the Scriptures *are* the sum of those propositions, whether they can be grasped in their *concrete* reality *in the logical way.* Quite apart from the fact that the Scriptures involve other than logical characteristics, e.g. aesthetic (so that to see them as merely logical propositions is to enlarge an aspect of them to be their whole), can we possibly account for what the Word of God claims for itself on this logistic (= scientific view of logic) reading? E.g. that it is a power to convert the soul? Do logical judgments, or any series of them, do that?

The logicistic thinker may offer as a rejoinder that he is thinking of the *truth* in logical proposition, and that a proper understanding of his meaning obviates the difficulty since the power is in the truth. But the next question is, What is that truth in the propositions? Is it the propositions?

The contemporary philosopher Martin Heidegger has vividly brought to our attention that 'truth' manifests itself in other ways than propositions. The truth of a work of art, for example, does not consist in a proposition or in any group of propositions. Barrett, in discussing the matter in his book *Irrational Man* (p. 192), writes: "The momentous assertion that Heidegger makes is that truth does not reside primarily in the intellect, but that, on the contrary, intellectual truth is in fact a derivative of a more basic" — I would add: and integral — "sense of truth".

Barrett presents us with a very clear illustration (*idem*, p. 198) of Heidegger's meaning. Someone tells me a new "theory" of his. It happens that as soon as I hear it I know it to be false. "Challenged to give arguments against it, I may stumble inarticulately; in some cases, indeed, I find it not worth-while to give a rebuttal, for the ideas ring false the moment they strike my ear. Some dumb inarticulated understanding, some sense of truth planted, as it were, in the marrow of my bones, makes me know that what I am hearing is not true. Whence comes this understanding? It is the understanding that I have by virtue of being rooted in existence. It is the kind of understanding we all have when confronted with ideas that we know to be false even though it may take us a long time to articulate reasons for rejecting them. If we did not have this understanding, we could never utter any propositions as true or false."

The logicistic thinker has lost his hold upon this primordial form of understanding. For him the central personal experiencing of truth has come to be reduced to one (logical) mode of this experiencing. But to identify the figures of a certain scientific mode of experiencing with the full concrete experience of life is precisely scientism.

In such logicism an internal problem still lurks. For logical figures contain in themselves a number of analogical moments. Within the 'world' of logic we speak of such 'things' as logical space — what the Germans call *Denkraum,* logical movement of thought (logical causality), logical thought-*life,* logical control (we say of someone that he has logical control of his material), logical commerce, logical economy of thought, logical harmony, logical eros (Platonic love), and so on. The presence of these analogical moments in our logical life would seem to indicate that 'the logical' does not stand by itself, and therefore cannot be equated with full concrete reality.

A Further Discussion of Logicism

But I wish to press my argument a step further in order to show as clearly as I can here the difficulties one runs into when attempting to explain the world of reality from the logical point of view. In logic since the time of Hume, and particularly of Kant, a great deal of attention has been given to what is called the logical difference between Is and Ought, between Sein and Sollen. We distinguish a proposition of the 'is' form (i.e. one of which the predicate is expressed by the words 'is' or 'will be' or their equivalent) from one of the 'ought' form (of which the predicate is expressed by the words 'ought' or 'should be' or an equivalent). Recently I participated in a discussion with a christian friend of mine who is much absorbed in logical questions. This question of the logical difference between 'is' and 'ought' came up, and my friend came up with a sentence to illustrate each. For the 'ought' statement he offered: "Thou shalt not kill"; for the 'is' statement: "God is the creator of the world, including me". Now I am not concerned to bring up all the details of our argument this morning. I want to make just one point. I granted my friend that there was a difference between the *logical forms* of the two statements, but I argued that merely this difference in logical form could not express a *deeper sense* in which his second statement — viz. God is the creator of the world, including me — could not be considered a statement of 'is' as *opposed to* a statement of 'ought'. I reminded him of what Calvin says about our knowledge of God in the second chapter of the first book of his *Institutio*. E.g. this: "For we cannot with propriety say there is any knowledge of God where there is no religion or piety", to which we must add the following from the second section of the same chapter: "See, then, the nature of pure and genuine religion. It consists in faith, united with a serious fear of God, comprehending a voluntary reverence, and producing legitimate worship agreeable to the injunctions of the law."

What was I trying to do by thus citing Calvin? I was trying to suggest to my friend that we must ask ourselves how we have come by the knowledge contained in the statement: "God is the creator of the world, including me," and, that if we do not ask ourselves that question we shall find ourselves involved in an *impasse*. For we can know this statement only by religion, and religion means "sensing" — not the modal psychical sensing, but the concrete religious awareness of the full man — my obligation of obedience to my sovereign God in terms of His Law. My knowledge that God is the creator of the world, including me, is not just a logical proposition or a lingual statement; it is *personal* knowledge, *heart*-knowledge: it is immediately gained by the total person whose heart is in the grip of the Word of God.

My logicistic friend was not really dealing with 'is' and 'ought', but only with these *in the way they are expressed in propositions*. When he limits his understanding of such matters to the peculiarly logical mode of experiencing them, he is seeing life merely in terms of its logico-lingual aspects, and thus of necessity making the relative abstract figures of logical structure to be the equivalent of life in its fulness. This is another instance of scientism, and is doomed to failure. Even for the person engaging in it the consequences are bad: if in the scientistic attitude we heartily embrace a particular aspect of life and attempt to understand the latter from out of the former, we shall find that we can no longer understand the Word of God.

This is, in my opinion, what was involved in the so-called Clark case in the Orthodox Presbyterian Church more than fifteen years ago.

Scientism in Theology

My third and final example of the scientistic attitude that we find all about us is taken from the world of theology. It is a very simple but *telling* example. Recently there has been some discussion in Christian Reformed circles about the proper grounds for erecting Christian schools. The traditional ground, it has been suggested by some, is the doctrine of the covenant. Again, I am not interested this morning in deciding whether this is the proper ground for our Christian schools. As a matter of fact, I doubt whether we can approach the problem even in this way, speaking of "a doctrine" as the ground. I suspect that a particular form of scientism is already present here, viz. theo-logicism or theologism — truth as so many disparate true theological propositions—, and I would suggest that our schools are based on the Truth of the divine word-revelation, which is one. But that is merely an 'aside'.

What I want to discuss more particularly right now is the culpable way in which one of the ministers of the Christian Reformed Church goes about rejecting the so-called 'doctrine' of the covenant as the suggested ground for the erection of our schools and the equally culpable way in which one of our educators goes about defending it. I am referring to the debate between the

Rev. Hugh Koops and Mr. Raymond Geerdes as recorded in the March, 1959 issue of *Torch and Trumpet*. Perhaps the quickest way to get into this debate is to quote a number of passages. Mr. Koops suggests that Mr. Geerdes is unhelpful because he "has looked for a foundation for a separate school system in the wrong area. He has turned to Christian theology and come up with the doctrine of the covenant". He then asks, "Is Christian education so bankrupt that it must turn to *another discipline* (italics mine) to find a foundation for our schools?" Further on he says that it grieves him that "an educator like Mr. Geerdes can find no educational ground for our school system, and must take recourse to what must be shaky ground for him". (He means theology, as a 'discipline' Mr. Geerdes presumably has not studied, and in which he would therefore probably not be at home.) He finally admonishes: "Let (Christian educators) define Christian education in educational rather than in theological principles . . . for the covenant belongs in the church, not in the school; in theology, not education; in the recreative, not the creative sphere." (At the mention of this last pair of concepts I am strongly tempted to cry out, "Oh, my poor aching head!" But I shall try to keep calm a while longer. For surely Mr. Koops' adversary will set things right?)

No; he does not. He writes: "Our theological heritage is a rich mine *with education implications*". (The familiar scholastic idea of theological *Lehnsätze* for the educational theory of the Christian, instead of an integral scripturally directed paedagogics.) He refers to what his opponent had said about theology's being shaky ground for an educator, calls it presumptuous of Mr. Koops, and, somewhat grandiloquently continues: "The ground that to the Rev. Koops is shaking earth is to me the *terra firma* of God's truth". Now, that sounds a little better; for Mr. Geerdes finally gets around to speaking of God's truth. But later he goes on to speak of theology. Now, which does he mean? For he must choose. Surely, the *terra firma* of God's truth ought not to be called theology, or we might get an unfortunate canonization, no, worse, declaration of infallibility of Berkhof or some other theologian (depending of course, on my hearers' preferences). Let us not be the cause of any theologian's becoming a stuffed shirt. As a science theology is like any other area of the scientific enterprise. Geerdes finishes by saying, "The issue is now before us. Is our distinctive Reformed theology the fountainhead of our Christian schools? Or is some solely "educational" discipline the justification for our schools?

The future of our schools in the second half of the Twentieth Century depends upon how we answer this question."

Religious Knowledge Not Theology

You are correct, Mr. Geerdes. Except that we must never answer it by accepting your disjunction. Our choice is fortunately not between theology and education. How can you put theology *over against* education if you mean by theology the Word of God? Indeed, the Word of God which makes us aware of the *reality* of the covenant and of much more is the renewing Word which makes both our theology and our education new. But both you men have confused the issue by identifying our knowledge of God with theology. If they were identical, how could our theology continue to be reformed, i.e. continue to reform itself? By what standard or Norm?

What we have here is an especially insidious form of scientism which makes the knowledge of the realities of God and creation and man equivalent to a theological statement about them. This confusion is to be found all about us. But the Reformation taught us that men are free from the theologians in understanding and interpreting the Word of God. Life precedes science, and in life God makes us aware of (reveals to us) the Truth. The theological expression, the educational expression, *all* scientific expression follows, and is informed by the deeper pre-scientific knowledge of the Truth that man does not have as a scientist but as man of God. It would seem that our Reformed circles are often far from the Reformation. The best thing you can read on this is the group of three chapters entitled "Philosophy and Theology" in the book *In the Twilight of Western Thought* by Herman Dooyeweerd (read esp. p. 135, 136, 144, 145).

Prof. T. F. Torrance of Edinburgh made himself guilty of the same theologistic error when he spoke to a gathering of faculty members at Calvin College a little over a year ago. In answering a question I had put to him he said that the empirical sciences by their very nature cannot tell about wholeness, but theology does just that: it tells us about wholeness. He did not explain how that could then be a science. The difference, he said, was the problem, for example, of the psychiatrist and the minister. The psychiatrist has some truth, he declared, but to know a man we need the wholeness of theology.

This Difference Known to Kuyper

The distinction between a knowledge of the Truth and theological knowledge was known also to Abraham Kuyper, who once wrote, "Just name the one name of Jesus Christ and you feel at once how the entire scientific enterprise must abandon its demand to take first place in our estimation of our life". Kuyper saw that a distinction had to be made between "the knowledge of God, which every one of the Lord's children possesses and which is eternal life", and "scientific theology, which is practiced in our faculties of theology." (See *De Heraut* No. 939; 22 Dec. 1895.)

With that I bring to an end my illustrations of the scientistic attitude of mind. Of course, these examples could be multiplied many times over. Wherever political scientists or linguists attempt to set the bounds of life-phenomena or to call life-forms into being (Esperanto), wherever people leave it to the theologians to figure out what we should believe, wherever the psychologist or the student of ethics claims that his science treats the whole of human behaviour, wherever Marxism prevails, — in all these places we have to do with the banal distortions of life caused by the attitudes of scientism.

Recognition of 'Pre-Scientific' Had To Come

Not only because of the awakening of the German professors but for many other reasons a change had to come. E.g., while at Harvard I had a friend who was a physicist. He had the scientistic bug, and we argued many times about it. Once on a picnic we were surprised by a sudden evening shower. My friend turned to his wife and said, "Let's get into the car and get home; after this the sun will soon be going down." In complete astonishment I, who had been standing idly by, came to full attention and, looking him straight in the eye, said, "Isn't that a disgrace that an intelligent scientist like you should condescend to use such *unscientific* language?" I offer this as an illustration of the fact that a scientistic scientist of necessity makes use of everyday language which does not have any scientific pretention whatsoever. To speak of the sun's going down is not *un*scientific; it is not a failure to be up to the scientific standard, not a *primitive* scientific statement. For it has nothing whatsoever to do with the scientific frame of mind. The *pre*-scientific is not *un*scientific but *non*-scientific; it

~~is of another kind than~~ scientific. A statement about the sunset does not refer to the earth and the sun in their mutual relations as a result of their physical motion in space; it is language which gives expression to our experience of life from out of our central (religious) human position as lords of the creation (Ps. 8). All the arguments about no longer being able to believe that man is the center of the created world and the earth the scene of the great drama of the covenantal fellowship between God and men stem from making the physical *aspect* of life the whole of life. But the physical aspect is *not* the whole, nor is the jural, nor is the logical, nor the biotic, nor any other aspect. Life in its totality, in its robust concrete meaning, is religion. But I shall not develop this theme until later.

Contemporary Evidences of a Changed Attitude

There had to come a change; there had to come a greater appreciation of everyday life. And there has. I do not say that there has come a *proper understanding* of pre-scientific life. But in the twentieth century there is everywhere noticeable a renewed interest in the pre-scientific, and a greater appreciation of the fundamental importance of understanding it if we are to plumb the mystery of our life. One of the traces of truth in all our present-day irrationalisms is that life is more basic than science, that science is the servant of life. But the general switch-about that I am referring to is by no means limited to irrationalistic philosophies. Let me suggest a few of the significant changes I have in mind.

Gestalt Psychology

I suppose in one sense we might begin with Von Ehrenfels' famous article of 1890, "Ueber Gestaltqualitäten" (which goes back to Ernst Mach), with Wertheimer, Koffka, Köhler, and the beginnings of the *Gestalt* school of psychology; for this school broke in some sense with the idea that everyday experience must be broken down into elements and then theoretically re-constructed, and drew attention to direct experience of persons and things. But that was only a beginning.

Lévy-Bruhl Abandons 'Pre-logical'

I have in mind, rather, to speak first of the famous French

anthropologist of the Sorbonne who died just at the outbreak of the Second World War, Lucien Lévy-Bruhl. (If ever there was a positivist, i.e. a thoroughly scientistic thinker, Lévy-Bruhl was it.) You have all heard, I am sure, of the positivistic dictum of the three stages in the evolution of the human understanding: the theological, metaphysical and positive scientific stages. Basing himself on this doctrine, Lévy-Bruhl produced a famous study of the primitive or pre-logical or mystical character of the thinking of primitive peoples. But in 1938 Lévy-Bruhl abandoned his distinction between 'pre-logical' and 'logical' (his recantation was published only posthumously in 1947, and is discussed by W. F. Albright in the 1951 French translation of his book, *From the Stone Age to Christianity*) precisely because, as Albright states it, "he found so much evidence of quite logical thinking in the ordinary affairs of life, even in the most primitive tribes of today".

Phenomenological and Existentialist 'Psychology'

The next thing I shall mention is the great development, since Brentano's doctrine of intentionality influenced Edmund Husserl, of phenomenological and existentialist psychology. Here too a much greater emphasis is being placed on concrete events and men in contact with things and persons. (The student may consult for this J. H. van den Berg, *Kroniek der Psychologie*, Boekencentrum N.V., 's-Gravenhage, 1953.)

Interest in Pre-scientific Language

The last thing I wish to mention is the increased interest in ordinary language that characterizes G. E. Moore, the later Wittgenstein, and certain currents in the school of language analysis. To which I would add a reference to a very important recent article by Prof. John Wild of Harvard in the *Philosophical Review,* entitled "Is there a World of Ordinary Language?" In that article Wild says that a "concern to achieve an accurate description of the concrete phenomena of the *Lebenswelt,* as they are experienced and expressed in ordinary language, is a constant theme of all Husserl's writings", and adds that "in this broad sense the influence of phenomenology has spread far and wide". He writes that "most European philosophers would agree that the task of describing the phenomena of this life-world and of analyzing its structure is of primary importance for philosophy". Wild was struck with the movement towards the concrete in both continental phenomenology and Anglo-Saxon language analysis, and he asks whether both movements are not "approaching the same thing (concrete experience) from different angles?"

Some Dutch Voices

In The Netherlands Prof. C. A. van Peursen has written: "Abstractie en formalisering zijn grootse mogelijkheden de mens geschonken. Zij moeten echter telkens terug tot het werkelijke, concrete leven, tot de mens, die met de vinger iets aanwijst". And Ds. Okke Jager (*Uw Wil Geschiede*, p. 17): "Wij zijn nog te veel vastgegroeid aan de leugen, dat de wetenschappelijke gedachtengang als zodanig helderder en nauwkeuriger is dan de niet-wetenschappelijke gedachtengang van iemand, die bidt."

That is enough, I think, to indicate something of the momentous re-orientation that has been and is still going on in the intellectual world of the twentieth century.

Recapitulation: Basic Problem of Scientism

It is time to draw together the sense of our discussion thus far and to take a somewhat closer, though necessarily brief and only suggestive, look at the fundamental problem involved in it. The problem which the long dominance of the scientistic frame of mind forces upon us is that of the relation that exists between what is properly called 'scientific' and what we may speak of as the 'pre-scientific'. Scientism recognizes only the scientific. It regards what we call 'pre-scientific' as *un*scientific, as something that falls short of meeting scientific specifications. It fails to observe that the 'pre-scientific' is not really *un*scientific, but rather *non*-scientific, i.e. *of a wholly other kind than scientific,* and therefore to be judged by other standards than those for science. It overlooks the important fact that this *non*-scientific experience (and knowledge) is also actually *pre*-scientific since it is always experience previous to the scientific, is indeed a necessary condition for the acquisition of it. In the Christian world a particularly striking example of the insidious working of the scientistic frame of mind is the confusion of the immediate awareness of the integral Truth of the Word of God in our hearts (God, of course, opening our hearts to believe His Word, cf. *Acts* 16:14) with a scientific (theological) body of propositional statements about this Truth. So much attention has been devoted to the latter that the necessary earlier possession of the former has largely been overlooked, to the great detriment, not least, of a proper understanding of theology *qua* science, of theological method in general, and in particular of the process of exegesis.

By its very nature then the scientistic mind has everywhere been compelled to ignore the important role that this everyday (non- and pre-scientific) experience plays in our lives. Thus scientism fails to note something of the structure of the creation, and as a result is compelled to render a distorted account both of our experience and of the cosmos. The consequences, as we have seen, have been legion and grave.

Scientism's Unresolved Problems

When, scientistically, one allows only scientific knowledge, one is forced to seek the sense or meaning of life in such knowledge. At once, however, the scientistic thinker is confronted with a difficulty. For there are many sciences, and their subject-matters and methods are different. The scientistic mind being not limited to any one area of scientific knowledge, many scientific viewpoints vie with one another for the powerful position of central religious revelation of the Truth.

Because time after time men have thus attempted to oversee all of reality from one or another of these diverse scientific viewpoints, many -isms have arisen in the course of human speculation: materialism, naturalism, biologism or vitalism, psychologism, logicism, historicism (German, *Historismus* — what Dr. Reid is talking to us about in this Conference), economism (Marx), aestheticism, moralism, etc. The very diversity of scientific points of view should warn us that we do not have to do in the several forms of scientific knowledge with life in its *radical unity*, but only with various 'aspects' or 'sides' of life.

Still more, the occurrence in all of the sciences of elementary or basic concepts of an analogical kind (a phenomenon which cannot be explained as metaphorical use of language) should caution us against assuming that any one scientific area exists by itself as empirical reality. For these *analogical concepts* in the various sciences, like the analogical moments of the several modal aspects that constitute our experience and which guarantee the specific modal sense of the analogical concepts, *are the expression of an indissoluble coherence of meaning in an irreducible diversity of meaning. They presuppose a deeper unity of meaning.* If we do not experience this unity in some one or other of the bodies of scientific knowledge, where then?

(There is no time now to go further into this particular matter of analogy and analogical concepts in science, though it is fundamental. I merely suggest it here for the fulness of the account. Any of you who might be interested in pursuing the subject may consult, besides Dooyeweerd's *A New Critique of Theoretical Thought* (see the index volume *sub voc.* "Analogical Concepts", "Analogy") and his book *Vernieuwing en Bezinning,* especially his brochure which deals with this, "De Analogische Grondbegrippen der Vakwetenschappen en Hun Betrekking tot de Structuur van den Menselijken Ervaringshorizon", published in *Mededelingen der Koninklijke Nederlandse Akademie van Wetenschappen,* Afd. Letterkunde, Nieuwe Reeks, Deel 17, No. 6 (1954), by N.V. Noord-Hollandse Uitgevers Maatschappij, Amsterdam.)

The diversity of scientific points of view already suggests it, and the occurence of analogical concepts in each science strongly indicates it, but a consideration of how we come by our scientific knowledge makes abundantly clear that there is, previous to our scientific experience, *a more integral experience of reality,* i.e. an experience of reality in its *wholeness* of meaning. For scientific knowledge can only be acquired by a process of *abstraction from life as thus experienced in its wholeness.*

Error of Scientism Illustrated

A simple illustration will make the point unmistakably clear. A young surgeon early in the morning comes down to the hospital where he is to perform an operation. As he is about to enter the front door of the hospital he finds himself suddenly face to face with the man who had been his favorite professor in the medical school, a man who, though now retired, likes to linger about the hospital. For one second their eyes meet, they shake hands and exchange a few words and pass. A few hours later we discover our young surgeon in a nearby dining room waiting for a couple of his colleagues to arrive. He is sitting at the table lost in thought. He is, in fact, thinking of his brief early-morning encounter with old 'Doc' Maguire. The old man, so our young surgeon is thinking to himself, still cuts quite a figure. In spite of his years he still walks sturdily, appears firm, has eyes like flint; he remains still a 'warm' personality, with eyes that literally draw you to him. Our surgeon smiles faintly to himself as he recalls his renewed experience of the incisiveness of the old man's eyes, something which in the old days had provoked frequent student comment. And again this morning, our surgeon muses, he had had repeated his sense of something unusually harmonious and pleasing about the professor's presence; and then, of course, also his gregariousness.

You will have noticed that in the dining room it takes our surgeon a long time to 'recount' what he experienced in but a moment of time early in the morning at the front door of the hospital. Further, at the table the surgeon is able to distinguish a number of 'sides' or 'aspects' to his 'experience' of old 'Doc' Maguire. At the moment of their meeting he was not strictly aware of any such diversity of aspects; he had simply experienced the 'Doc'. Yet *if he had not experienced them in the morning he would not have been able to recall them as experienced at noon.* But there they were. The eyes like flint (organic). The warm personality and drawing eyes (psychical). The piercing or incisive look (logical). The gregariousness (social). The pleasing harmony (æsthetic). In the morning these aspects had been experienced only *implicitly;* at noon, *explicitly.*

These several aspects become the fields of investigation of the special sciences. The science of the organic, for example, disentangles (abstracts) from its interwovenness in the whole concrete experience that which is peculiarly organic, that which is subject to *organic* laws. Psychology does the same thing (or should) with 'the psychical'; logic or analytics, with 'the analytical'; æsthetics, with 'the æsthetic'.

In daily life, however, we experience persons like 'Doc' Maguire, things, events and institutions *concretely,* i.e. in the wholeness of their meaning. The tree on the hill, under which the young man chooses to picnic with his beloved, is for that youth 'good' not only in the biotic sense, but also psychically, socially, æsthetically, etc. But our youth is not aware of all these distinctions. (As soon as he is he abandons, for a moment, the everyday attitude.) Rather, he grasps the 'sense' of the situation integrally. This kind of experience is presupposed in the later scientistic abstraction; it is thus not only non-scientific but also pre-scientific. This common or everyday experience we call *naive experience* (from Latin, *nativum,* meaning 'original').

Another Illustration

A second illustration may serve to bring into still sharper focus the relation of scientific knowledge to naive experience. Imagine a modern coffee shop so enclosed within a glass wall that we who are without can see and hear what is going on inside without being detected. Inside, life is going on as is usual in such a coffee shop. But let us suppose that we have lined up around the outside of the glass wall a group of scientists intent on observing the life within. Let us say that among them are a physicist, a biologist, a logician, a linguist, a student of social life, an economist and a student of æsthetics. All these scientists observe the same life-situations: some people inside are standing at the counter ordering; others are sitting at tables alone or in groups, the latter engaged in quiet or animated conversation. But out of this whole situation, which each scientist experiences, the physicist, for example, abstracts only those 'figures' that tell something about mass, motion, force, etc., such as the work involved in lifting a cup of coffee from the table-top to the mouth against the pull of gravity. Other than figures of this kind he utterly ignores *as physicist*. At the same time that our physicist is doing this the biologist watches for such things as the return of 'life' to the exhausted body, digestion, etc. He ignores the physical and other 'figures' the other scientists are raptly observing. The logician listens for logical 'figures' of implication in the often enthymemic reasoning of everyday life. The linguist abstracts those 'moments' that have something to tell him about human symbolical communication. The student of social life is watching for social *mores;* he may be studying the very same gestures the linguist is watching, but rather from the standpoint of ways of persons' getting along with one another than from the standpoint of symbolical communication. The economist notices how large a cup of coffee you can buy for the price paid, and for signs of the 'market's' willingness or unwillingness to pay. (Note that when we speak of the people on the floor of the stock-exchange — or, for that matter, the people assembled at an old European village market — as 'market' we are using a term which describes that human situation there (Human Society) not in its *wholeness* of meaning, but only from the economic point of view: a lover might have arranged a rendezvous with his beloved in the centre of the flower-market, but this is not 'market'.) Finally, the student of æsthetics will be observing in the life that is playing itself off inside the coffee shop what is pleasing and harmonious in the gestures, movements, arrangements, etc. He too is abstracting 'figures'.

These illustrations, I think, make sufficiently clear why we must not, scientistically, seek the unity and meaning of life in any body of scientific knowledge. The sciences arise from the fact that there are various *ways* (Latin, *modus;* Engl. modes, hence, modalities) of viewing the one reality, and every special science deals with only a 'facet' of life.

Wholeness of Life Given in Naive Experience

Life itself we meet only in our naive experience. Here we experience not only persons and things, events and institutions in their wholeness, but also the *given* interwovenness of all these in their subject-subject and subject-object relations. (See *Christian Perspectives, 1960,* p. 128 f.) By way of our naive experience we grasp something of the sense of reality as a whole, sense something of the unity of life.

For this reason, as we have seen, much contemporary thought is now attempting to find the meaning of life in everyday situations. William Barrett, for instance, in his book *Irrational Man* (which you should read), says that existentialism "seeks to bring the whole man — the concrete individual in the whole context of his everyday life, and in his total mystery and questionableness — into philosophy". The notion is abroad today that life is to be explained in terms of concrete encounters. We read frequently that the encounter between human persons is more important than our scientific knowledge of things. Love, it is often maintained, will show us the meaning of life.

Yet, Sense of Life Elusory

Praiseworthy as is the turn to naive experience, the attempt now to find in it the unity and meaning of our existence is doomed to failure just as certainly as was the earlier scientistic adventure. As long as men seek this unity and meaning within our functional life, it will elude them, for the simple reason that throughout all the reaches of this functional life there constantly reappears a modal *diversity* of meaning. Love itself, for instance, displays many senses. There is erotic or sexual love, marital love, filial and parental love, love of one's country (patriotism), love for rational distinction (platonic love), the love of beauty, the love of the brethren in the instituted church, and so on. Where in all this diversity is the unified sense of our existence that men seek?

We have previously seen that in the irreducible *diversity* of meaning that an analysis of our experience everywhere discloses there is an indissoluble *coherence* of meaning, which presupposes a deeper *unity* of meaning, a concentration, as it were, of all the diverse 'sides' of meaning. But what this unity might be no examination into our functional life can discover. At this point we reach the limits of an analytical examination of our experience.

Scriptural Insight into Life as Religion

Only when the living and powerful Word of God, about which I talked to you in the lectures last year, takes hold of us in our hearts and unites us to Christ can we know the Truth.[1] Only then are men made to 'see', to see the unity of meaning in the diversity and coherence. Only then are we made aware of our office as men, the office of being servants of God in singleness of heart; only then are we made aware of our central position in the cosmos, a central position where all the 'aspects' of our created life are concentrated in the meaning of life as religion.

The Truth, as the divine Word discloses it, is that *life is religion*. No, I did not say 'religious'. To say that need only mean that 'religion' is one dimension of created reality among many, as when we say that life is beautiful. When I use the noun and say that life is religion I mean to say that religion is the concentration-point of all the 'sides' or 'aspects' of created meaning. To take our example of love, we shall remain floundering in a temporal diversity of meaning until we see in the great (religious) commandment

---

[1] See above, p. 32 f., 39 ff.

to love the Lord our God with our whole heart the concentration and fulfillment of the diverse modal 'aspects' of love.) Likewise, all our words receive in religion their unity and fulfillment. Take the word 'world'. We may speak of a physical world, of the world of life, the world of sense, the economic world or the world of beauty, but by now we are able to see that in each of these instances the word 'world' should be enclosed within quotation marks. For each of these 'worlds' is but an aspect of the concrete world, the world in its fulness of meaning. It was simply the prophet in man, a condition of human existence that as such remains — though (immanentistically) mis-directed — in the fallen state, which caused men in their spiritual blindness to identify first one and then another of these 'worlds' with the world. Reality is neither the physical 'world' nor the 'world' of beauty, nor any other such 'world', but is that wonderful covenant fellowship which God has established with man, who (now in Christ) occupies the central place in the creation, who is put under the divine Law in the three-fold office of prophet-priest-king to worship and serve God in carrying out the cultural mandate in the world in singleness of heart.

Beneficial Fruits of a Scriptural Insight

The man who has seen life as religion can never again fall back into being a mere 'scientific mind' (absent-minded professor). He is on the way to becoming that perfect man of God, thoroughly furnished unto every good work, about whom Paul writes in II Tim. 3:17. That young Christian students see this is a matter of life or death for the Body of Christ in our time. And not only that they see it, but that they whole-heartedly believe it and live in accordance with it. For it is, after all, nothing but the Gospel, and the Gospel is our full salvation in the world, thus also in the 'world' of the university. To believe the Gospel is to be saved from unbelief and its fruits: revolution and disintegration.

Devastations Wrought by Scientism

The lamentable fact is that many Christians who pass through our universities get bitten by the bug of scientism. We must never forget that scientism is itself a belief, a faith.

That is, it offers itself, just as all faiths do, as the directing Principle of human life. But scientism is a false faith; its direction has been mis-direction. All who suffer its infection lose their way, Christians as well as non-Christians.

Those Christians who might have used a truly Christian university education to discover how to relate simple Christian faith to the cultural situation of our time and thus been enabled to enter into discussion with the Bertrand Russells of the world have themselves become sidetracked. Some of them get caught up in the mathematical-physical way (method) of viewing experience; others, in the biological, or psychological, or whatever. Either they become so completely absorbed in their area of specialization that in their personal lives they retreat from the fulness of life and of manhood to become sad examples of that strange 'lost' soul, the abstract scientific mind, or perhaps they attempt to 'see' (i.e. oversee) all of life from the special point of view of their field of study and come sooner or later to present much-demanded lectures on how 'the physicist' or 'the biologist' or the what-have-you looks at life, or, at the very best, in addition to their studies in the special science of their choice they find some time also for *theological* questions and theological *Lehnsätze*.

Each of these ways of behaviour suffers from the sickness of scientism — the third no less than the others — and sidetracks the Christian from carrying out his task in the world. The substitution of theology for a central religious awareness of the Truth is a very effective way of cutting the Christian religion down to scientistic size. It is just one more way of missing the central religious meaning of life. To add theological disquisitions to biological or psychological or sociological ones does not bring us one whit closer to the root-unity of life or to the Truth.

Our Task

What must be re-discovered in Protestantism if we are to survive in the gigantic cultural struggle of our time is an awareness of the directing role in life of the Word of God, the *sense* of that Word. To a more positively articulated statement about that we shall come in the next lecture. In the present lecture we have had first to clear the path by discussing that scientism which has so universally sidetracked Christians from the way to wisdom and abundant life.

Lecture V

Sphere-Sovereignty

Some time ago an address was delivered in Washington, D.C. in which a distinguished man had this to say: "In an industrial society men have to work out a great part of their destiny within the framework of business or industry, and these will have to provide much more than just the business services they render." As an illustration of what he meant the speaker pointed to the medieval guilds.

I refer to the incident here only to make clear that the influence of scientism still pervades our life. How could it ever be proper to speak of an *industrial SOCIETY?* Is there in society not also the life of married couples, are there not families and church-institutes, the arts, schools, and, last but scarcely least, the state? And do we not mean when we speak of human society the human community in its totality of possible relations, or all the ways in which we live our lives in community with our fellow-men? How then could a whole society come to be known as an *industrial* society?

You reply, "But this concept is merely meant to be a *description* of a particular society we find before us, in which the economic and technical sides of life have grown to be dominant, just as we might speak of the society of the Middle Ages as an ecclesiasticized society". Let me point out then that the speaker we have cited speaks of an industrial society in which "men have to work out a great part of their destiny within the framework of business or industry" and that he argues that "these will have to provide much more than just the business services they render".

Are Facts Normed?

Must we, as this speaker does, *accept* the fact of a society that is coming to be dominated by technology and industry as the point of departure for our thinking about what must be done in society? Let it be granted that business, technology and industry do take up an unusually large part of our lives in our society. Can this be regarded as anything but a most *abnormal* situation? Would such a development have taken place if the lives of our marriages and families, of our churches and our states, if our social life and the life of the arts and sciences among us had been sound? But if our society is sick, should we accommodate to it, or, as in the case of bodily sickness, intervene, either by surgical removal or by stimulating other powers latent in the body, in order to combat the disease?

Is there a 'Pou Sto'?

Of course, intervention, at least meaningful intervention, supposes an insight into what a healthy order would be. Do we possess anywhere such an insight? If we do not, are we not compelled just to accept the fact of an industrial society, and attempt to solve our problems within the possibilities it provides us? But if we do, what central reality is it from out of which we can properly oversee human society in all the complexity of its functional life? Is there a point somewhere out beyond, not itself immanently involved in our functional existence, to which we can withdraw and from which we can attain to such an overview, in order that we may return within the order of our society to judge its relative sickness or health and to work to rectify what is not good?

My young friends, this is the problem, in its solution so gravely momentous for all mankind, to which the concept of sphere-sovereignty claims to give a scriptural answer.

Only when we have reached the point to which our first lecture brought us are we at all in a position to understand and judge the significance of the debate about sphere-sovereignty. We had to be rid of the attitude of scientism in order to see life as religion. Scientism cannot allow any order or structure in temporal reality that is not the product of scientific reflection, the only Oracle or Source of truth it recognizes. Yet scientific thought, by its very abstracting nature, is compelled to remain enclosed within some one or other aspect of temporal reality. It thus must lack the *point d'appui* or central vantage-point from which a view of the whole of life in its order or structure can be had. This is already to be seen from the conflicting diversity of points of view to which scientism has given rise. No science, no scientific point of view, not even that of theology, can give us the central insight we need into the order of society. Such an insight into an ordering principle can only be experienced when, by reason of the hold that the Word of God takes upon them, our hearts have been opened to the religious root-life of the temporal world. Only in religion, which is, after all, our ultimate human situation, only when we stand in Christ, the Truth, do we become aware of the principle of sphere-sovereignty.

But when we have seen what it means to say that our life is religion, when we have seen Christ as the new Root and Head of recreated humanity, to whom, as the Ruler of society, all power has been given, then we will also understand sphere-sovereignty. That is how it went with Abraham Kuyper, the man with whose name you undoubtedly connect this concept. In the manner of a new and living faith Kuyper saw *the place of Christ within the creation-order of God* as the new Office-bearer in Adam's stead. But then the vast and life-quickening perspectives of sphere-sovereignty at once opened themselves up to him. Sphere-sovereignty became for Kuyper the expression of the Order of Creation as graciously revealed to us anew in the Word of God. So intimately was sphere-sovereignty bound up with his central insight into the Word of God that Kuyper made it the fundamental principle of his Anti-revolutionary political action. And on that "day of days in Kuyper's life" as Mr. VandenBerg in his recent book, *Abraham Kuyper,* so fittingly describes the momentous opening day of the Free University of Amsterdam, Kuyper spoke in his opening address on . . . sphere-sovereignty.

Statement of Thesis

The central thesis of my lecture this morning is that the concept of sphere-sovereignty gives accurate expression to the scriptural revelation about the structural "bouw" or make-up of created reality and that it thus becomes, as the meaning of the divine word-revelation, our Arché, the Principle or Starting-point which drives, directs and governs all our life-activities in the world.

To discuss sphere-sovereignty is at once as simple and as extraordinarily difficult as any subject could be. In one sense I can frankly tell you that I did not choose this topic for these lectures; it chose me. In the light of the perilous situation of all mankind in our time and of the absence of insight and conviction on the part of Christians I felt that we shall have to come to think more seriously about this subject, not only privately, but especially in a collective way. I know that I shall not be able to rise to the heights that my subject demands; I only wish to stimulate your collective thinking about the matter. It would be impossible in one lecture thoroughly to argue sphere-sovereignty. Right now I am merely presenting it for your consideration. I trust it will send you to the books and articles. That is what I take to be one of the main purposes of this Conference: to stimulate a further collective study and reflection on certain crucial (central) problems to which we shall in the future have to give a collective answer. We must create among us a "denkgemeenschap", a community of thought. For just this purpose an Institute which could give continuous opportunity for such directed communal thinking ought to be set up at the earliest possible date. Time and events press us.

Its Contemporary Importance

It will not be necessary for us to return to Abraham Kuyper and The Netherlands of the last century in order to feel the surpassing importance of our present theme. In our own time and place the question that is perhaps uppermost in the thoughts and conversations of concerned men everywhere is the question about the nature and limits of authority; it is undoubtedly the most urgent question facing our democracies. How is government related to business, industry and technology? What is the relation of a trade-union to a political party (a particularly pressing question at the moment here in Canada, but scarcely less so in the United States)? What relation should exist between the church and education, between the government and education (e.g. when a government, as in the U.S.A. recently, suddenly faces the need, for the preservation of its national existence, to have the schools in the nation catch up with the standards of their Russian counterparts), between religion and education? What but fear of conflict of authority can explain the concern that is felt about having a Roman Catholic president? What are we to think of a political party that openly bases itself on a religious — I did not say ecclesiastical — credo? Just what may a minister of the Word of God say from the pulpit about political and social matters? What is the responsibility of the government to the arts, and in general with respect to the cultural development of its people? Why do we abhor Red China's communes and the interference they represent in the life of China's families?

The consistent modern mind should see no difficulty in experimenting in any way that men themselves might wish. Men have only to follow the dictates of their own (and the only) inner guide of reason in order to achieve the earthly kingdom of blessedness. The will of the people is the only will of God we can know. *Vox populi vox Dei.* Therefore, experiment to your heart's — no, to your mind's — content. (Note that our problem, because it has to do with the limits of authority, has also to do with the Origin of authority. These are always but two facets of the one problem: structure and Origin always go together.) Such a view about the nature and limitlessness of authority is behind the communist experimentation. But that experimentation has had a history, not only in the West in the time of the French Revolution, but also in Russia in the early days of the Bolshevik regime, and the result was the discovery that 'something', some mysterious power appears to hem us in in our inordinate (ordo!) desire for endless experimentation; something seems to limit our exercise of our allegedly limitless power. Many shifts in the communist party line can be ascribed, as Vice President Richard Nixon said recently in a statement on the meaning of communism, "to the struggles of conscientious men trying to fit an inconvenient text to the facts of reality".

In spite of the difficulties they encounter the radical or consistent modern thinkers persist. And that is because they *believe.* To adopt a slogan that has been used in Dutch Reformed circles, these radicals are "looking to reason's commandment and blind to the outcome". That is the expression of their faith. The communist at least believes in his principle. Whittaker Chambers, who knew something about communism, put it this way in the *Letter to My Children* that constitutes the Foreword of his book *Witness:* "Communists are that part of mankind which has recovered the power to live or die — to bear witness — for its faith".

Chambers' use of the word 'recovered' calls us back to the realities of the situation in our western world. The weakness of the West is its inability to believe something. Unable to embrace any integral Christianity, the West, perhaps to a significant degree because of what yet is left of Christendom in the world, cannot with singleness of heart accept the faith of modern unbelief either. She is like Israel in the days of Elijah, limping between the two sides, critically weak. You will recall the nihilistic utterance of Bertrand Russell that I referred to in yesterday's lecture to the effect that men cannot discover a singly clear aim to be striven after or a single clear principle that might direct them. Since the West is neither cold nor hot, God will spew her out of His mouth. Unless she repent. But where is the West's Elijah, you ask? My young friends, we must not forget that Elijah belonged to the old dispensation; we belong to the new. God's Spirit has been poured out upon all flesh, and we — you and I — are the West's Elijahs. What do we have to prophesy?

Pseudo-Principles of Western Man

We must not think that western men have simply in their indolence decided that there is no Light to guide them. They have been treated to a whole series of Guiding Lights. The entire history of modern philosophy, until very recently, has been one frantically persistent search for some directing first principle.

Some, with Descartes, felt that by applying the method of radical doubt they could finally discover a body of innate or original ideas — *ideae innatae* — to which the name of *lumen naturale* — natural light, or light of (rational) nature — was given. A later twist of this view, influenced by an effete Christendom, was the notion of an absolute conscience, i.e. a conscience that can absolutely distinguish what is right and wrong. Another movement in the modern search for first principles, the one we know by the name of empiricism, thought that it had come up with certain absolutely ultimate, hard and irresistible "facts", known as sense-data. A fundamental difficulty is that even in John Locke (*Essay*, bk IV chapter I section 2) the word 'perception' bears a multivocal meaning (psychical meaning but also the logical meaning of analytical discernment).

We cannot go through this whole history at this time, but we must remember two things. These men had rejected the Word of God as the Source of certainty, truth and comfort. But they had not ceased to be 'believers': they had simply replaced the Scriptures with their own theoretical reason. These men were scientistic thinkers. They never found the firm Ground or sure Principle that they were seeking, and the principal cause of their failure was just that scientific attitude that we discussed at some length yesterday.

The failure to discover an absolute Beginning (Principle) has led many men to turn their attention away from beginnings towards consequences. William James described the method of pragmatism as the "attitude of looking away from first things, principles, 'categories', supposed necessities; and of looking towards last things, fruits, consequences, facts". This is very far removed from any awareness of a creation-structure or creation-order that is, in that other sense of the word, an order or command for our human life-activity. The upshot of our western history is that chilling nihilistic outcry of Lord Russell.[1]

Devastating Influence of Positivism

The positivistic movement, in particular, has had an unusually destructive influence upon men's insight into society: concentrating on the *positive forms* which the various societal structures have assumed in history, which always display a *changing* character, it has overlooked the constant and normative structural laws that God has ordained for our life. This led naturally to a complete levelling of inner structural differences between church and state, between marriage and companionship, etc. E.g. Harold Laski, in his *A Grammar of Politics* could not find any essential difference between the modern state and a federation of mine workers.

Prof. R. G. Collingwood in his book *The Idea of Nature* (p. 16) states the positivist case on this question very clearly. Speaking of the need for a "somewhat extensive reform in the vocabulary of natural science, such that all words and phrases descriptive of substance or structure shall be replaced by words and phrases descriptive of function", he writes further: "A mechanistic science of nature will already possess a considerable vocabulary of functional terms, but these will always be accompanied by another vocabulary of structural terms. In any machine structure is one thing, function another; for a machine has to be constructed

---

[1] See above, p. 93 f.

before it can be set in motion . . . to sum this up: in a machine, and therefore in nature if nature is mechanical, structure and function are distinct, and function presupposes structure. In the world of human affairs as known to the historian there is no such distinction and *a fortiori* no such priority. Structure is resolvable into function. There is no harm in historians talking about the structure of feudal society or of capitalist industry or of the Greek city-state, but the reason why there is no harm in it is because (!) they know that these so-called structures are really complexes of function, kinds of ways in which human beings behave . . . ."

Prof. Dooyeweerd has pointed out that the concept of function employed by the special sciences, which can only grasp the abstract functional relations of things and events within a particular aspect of reality, is not adequate to account for the concrete structures of individuality — e.g. state, church, marriage, family, labor union, etc. — that we experience in everyday life. A structure of individuality is a temporal *totality*-structure, in which *all aspects of the functional world are grouped in a typical way*. There is a constant order or structural grouping of functions. The positivistic point of view, which would allow only 'facts' to weigh with us, overlooks the decisive fact that those 'facts' are themselves only given to us in definite structures which find their ground not in human arbitrariness but in the divine world-order.

But I am getting a bit ahead of my story. Up to this point I have been concerned to picture — only very briefly and with reference to the point in question — the historical development of the West in order to show the *need* that our contemporaries have of a directing Principle. I have suggested further that it is impossible from a scientistic (e.g. positivistic) point of view to see the Order or Structure that pervades our life, and that that 'sight' only comes with the (divine) opening of our heart's eye to see our whole life as religion. But I have asserted that this particular in-'sight' does come with this revelation.

Present Status of Sphere-Sovereignty

Having said that, I must point out that there is a peculiar situation prevailing with respect to the status of the concept of sphere-sovereignty. In The Netherlands. Abraham Kuyper succeeded in the last quarter of the nineteenth century in making sphere-sovereignty a part of the conceptual apparatus of a great majority of the Reformed Christians of his country. Yet, in the Reformed world outside of The Netherlands, except where there has been an influx of Dutch Reformed influence, whether by immigration or otherwise, I dare say you would never hear the term. And not just the term; I suspect the idea itself would not be present, that is, not explicitly, except in a most reductivist sense (e.g. the relation of Church and State). I must qualify myself at this point and say that this has been the case until recently. For especially since the Second World War the vigorous, Scripture-fed thought of a number of Reformed thinkers in The Netherlands has begun to spill over into surrounding countries like Germany and France and Belgium, and indeed even to invade in a small way a number of the southern countries of Western Europe.

At the same time an opposite tendency is to be noted in American Reformed circles that derive from The Netherlands. Here an explicit rejection of sphere-sovereignty as in any sense a real principle is increasingly making itself heard in recent years. And in no uncertain language! It is widely known that a professor in a certain Calvinistic college has for a number of years been telling his students that sphere-sovereignty is a sacred cow which they would do well to throw out the window. Now I do not know whether that professor is a practical man. But I would suggest that it is not the simplest thing in the world to throw a cow out of the window. The year before I entered my college, I have been told, a number of upper classmen succeeded after much toil in placing a cow in the third floor study of one of their especially beloved professors. But it took pulleys and tackle and a lot of sweating firemen the next morning to get the cow out of that study window. Imagine how much more difficult the problem would have been if the cow had been sacred, i.e. untouchable. All joking aside, however, while the professor in question dared to say outright what he thought, and in his own peculiar way, there are many in our American circles who substantially agree with him. But I wonder if they really understand the position this inchoate rejection of sphere-sovereignty puts them in. For that same professor is reported to have said in the same connection that in a complex society all we can do is to nudge and see what happens. I would submit to you that this is essentially the way of life of the pragmatist faith, but also that there is *no other recourse if we are not in possession of a directing Principle.*

The Issue

Pragmatic or principled? Here, my dear young friends, is the greatest issue your generation has to face. The crisis of our age presses us to give an answer. Where are we? What is it to be a Christian, to lead a Christian life? What is it to possess the Word of God? Is there nothing left for us but to nudge, along with the other creeping specimens of our lowly human species, or are we able in Christ to stand in our Office — (calling) — as Man, and oversee what we are doing and what there is to do? Is it true that "the entrance of thy Word giveth light; it giveth understanding unto the simple" (Ps. 119:130)? Is it meaningful to pray "Teach me thy way, O Lord; I will walk in thy truth", together with what the psalmist wondrously immediately conjoins: "unite my heart to fear thy name" (Ps. 86:11), by which the essential connection between the seeing of the way to go and the seeing of the religious root-life of our existence is established?

Treachery of Traditionalism

Of course it is true; of course it is meaningful. We *are* men of a principle and we are not pragmatists. Yet I must here warn you that we may not permit ourselves simply to continue to repeat such pregnant phrases without the quickening insight of a living faith. Orthodoxy is not conservatism. Traditionalism is that quiet final stage of life that ushers in death.

In The Netherlands in the years following upon the death of Kuyper the concept of sphere-sovereignty underwent something of a diminution of meaning. It came to be a traditional parole, often passed on as scarcely more than the conventional symbol that marked off Kuyper's followers from other Netherlanders. The phrase came to mean merely a certain political doctrine and was no longer 'seen' as Kuyper had 'seen' it. Once thus degraded in meaning, it only took the steadily increasing confusions of a younger generation amid the multitudinous complexities of our twentieth-century life to induce many to dispense with sphere-sovereignty as one of those alleged 'principles' which the fertile brain of Kuyper had so liberally spilled out over the heads of the unsuspecting 'Kleine luyden'. No doubt this unfortunate development in The Netherlands has served to strengthen the sceptical tendency in Reformed circles of Dutch origin in America. But it was not, I think, the cause. The cause, I feel sure, was the same treacherous traditionalism that was also at work in Holland. Having to tackle the difficult problem of living in the United States, the generation that grew up here since the First World War became so involved in these problems that it gradually became very much estranged from its roots in Dutch reformed experience. Living by faith means living deeply involved and living at a distance at one and the same time. Men got too completely caught up in the immediacies of life. Gradually, this generation became uprooted from those great insights of faith that had been the source of their fathers' strength. In the meantime they had continued to pay lip-service to the old shibboleths, one of which was sphere-sovereignty. But this notion took on more and more of a hollow sound, and loosened itself from the on-going stream of life, much as an old protective covering that has outlived its usefulness is loosened from the living insect. Is it not just what you would expect that the day would come when the young American of Calvinist extraction would suddenly wake up and declare that sphere-sovereignty is meaningless? That is the treachery of traditionalism.

Revived Debate: Necessity of Decision

But then suddenly another voice, a voice with the certain sound of the trumpet, was heard in the languishing land. The men at the Free University who in the middle twenties initiated the movement for a scripturally-directed or Christocentric philosophy began to draw our attention in what seemed like a new and living way to the deep and central scriptural insight that is expressed in Kuyper's concept of sphere-sovereignty. Thus the issue is drawn and we must choose.

What, now, in the light of this confused situation I have just been describing, are we to think of sphere-sovereignty? Is it something peculiarly Dutch, that Reformed Christians of other nationalities are not familiar with it? Is it something peculiarly 19th century (or pre-World War I) that 20th century sons and daughters show so little feeling for it? When personally I say to you that in my estimation there is nothing that needs to be understood more than sphere-sovereignty if we are really to see our prophetic-priestly-kingly task in the world, then that is, of course, my privilege, and all well and good. It is a confession of my own faith, and I sincerely think that many of you will give it serious consideration. But ultimately I must show the *ground* of my faith. Then discussion becomes possible and a perspective opens up.

In the Reformed circles I am close to, I fear that we are often inclined to fall into what is really a species of subjectivism, which avoids the challenge of differing opinions by saying: "You have your opinion and I have mine and that's it." *We* are not the ultimate law; we are creatures, *under* the law. Thus we have no right to hold opinions that are not soundly grounded in an analysis, *in the light of the Word of God*, of lawful states of affairs. When we act as though we *do* have that right, we have made little gods of ourselves and discussion between supposed gods is precluded. When we do not test our opinions in debate and otherwise, and when we withdraw from making responsible decisions, we do not come farther. Life loses its dynamic quality; it shrivels up. Having made little gods of ourselves we lose the power to be men, that is MEN in the sense of the 'men of God' of the Scriptures. Yet God *made* us to be prophets, and we are *obliged* to speak the *truth*.

Why then do I believe as I do on this matter of sphere-sovereignty? What brought Kuyper to the idea? In what sense is sphere-sovereignty scriptural?

The Religious Place of Understanding

When we begin to discuss this subject we must not forget that life and human society are there, and need to be explained. There are marital unions between husbands and wives; there are family relationships, social ties and business connections, universities and scholarly associations, artists' colonies, and the like. And there is a complex interweaving of all of these in what would appear to be an 'order' suggesting some kind of an underlying unity. If we do not remember that life in all its variety is there first, we shall be in danger of falling into a scientistic frame of mind. The intellectual 'constructs' by which men attempt to 'see' or oversee in a single picture life and society do not themselves *constitute* that life and society. That world is there by virtue of the creation fiat, and has not only given rise to a long history of theoretical views of it, but has largely "defied" explanation. Yet the reason for this last fact is not that is has not been given to man to "see" his life and his world, but that man himself has not been standing in the right place to see it properly, that place where all the complex functions assume a meaningful place within the whole. That meaningful place is the *central* place; it is *religion:* man created and placed before God in a covenantal fellowship to render his Creator praise in a whole-hearted service of love and obedience within the length and breadth of the creation.

It may seem strange at first to some of you that I call religion a place. Of course, that does not mean a spatial place, because when I say religion is a place I mean something beyond all merely temporal aspects. It is with the word 'place' as we found it with the word 'up' yesterday. It is the bearer of many meanings; it is, as we say, multivocal, as opposed to univocal. It can have any number of modal meanings. For example, when my friend suddenly does something that hurts me I can say that there was no place for such an act, that it was not 'fitting'. I mean then an ethical 'place'; I mean that our friendship excludes what he did. Of a musical composition I can hold the opinion that some subordinate motif or part does not belong, does not have a place in the whole. Then I mean an aesthetic 'place'. When someone comes home from a formal banquet and complains that a certain person did not deserve his place at the main table he is speaking of a social 'place'. But besides all these modal meanings of the word 'place' there is that fulness or fulfilment of meaning of the word 'place' when we speak of place in its central religious sense. We must not forget what we said yesterday. The world is not the aesthetic 'world' or the 'world' of science or the 'world' of thought or the 'world' of economic life. These are all 'worlds'; the *world* is the concrete world that God created, headed by and centered in man, the world of God's wonderful covenant fellowship with us, the world in which all those modal 'worlds' assume a place. The fulness of meaning of the word 'world' can be understood only in religion, and so it is also with that word 'place'. The question "Where art thou?", which, by the way, God addresses not to Adam and Eve together but only to Adam, is not to be interpreted as "Behind which bush art thou?". It means that God did not find man in the place in which He had put him in the creation. This is the religious meaning of 'place' and is what I was referring to when I said that man cannot "see" or oversee the world and his life in their integral unity of meaning except as he stands in his place.

Sphere-Sovereignty and Integral Sense of Scripture

I therefore regard it as highly significant that the idea of sphere-sovereignty is so closely tied up with our recovery (from the scholasticism, i.e. theologism or scientism of the theologians) of what the Word of God tells us about the central religious nature of human life and society. In Abraham Kuyper this is especially clear. Where he is dealing strictly with questions that arise in the theological tradition Kuyper is not always at his best; the traditional theological motive of the natural and the supra-natural, a dualistic motive that cannot be harmonized with the scriptural revelation of the integral religious unity of man and the world, seems often to have been too powerful even for him. But in his discussion of matters that have to do with life and society in their concrete wholeness, matters which the theologians in their abstract study had left untouched, Kuyper is freed from the hold of traditional motives. Here he is close to the Scriptures, *and it is just in these areas of his thought that we notice the emergence of the idea of sphere-sovereignty*. As I have said, this idea is intimately bound up with the scriptural view that our life in its totality is religion.

Scriptural Themes in Kuyper: the Heart

Let me point to just one or two themes in Kuyper's thought that are related essentially to his recovery of this central meaning of the divine word-revelation. I think first of his radical break in principle — he did not everywhere achieve a breakthrough, not even in his *Encyclopedia* — with the scientism that was so characteristic of his time. He wrote, for example, in an article in *De Heraut* (no. 79; 15 Juni 1879) that according to the Word of God not the head but the heart is the means to knowledge. He specifically states — as if he might have foreseen the distortion of his meaning which some of his so-called 'followers' are even now busily propagating, a distortion which renders Kuyper's thought powerless — that he means by the heart not the organ of feeling, but that place in a man where God works, and from out of which He exercises an influence also upon the head and the brain. This recovery of the scriptural meaning of 'heart' is one element that simply cannot be missed if we are to understand once more what the Bible means by religion. It is therefore to be regretted that in a number of significant places in his famous Stone Lectures on Calvinism the English version has rendered Kuyper's 'hart' by 'mind'. In this way that for which we must be most grateful to Kuyper, viz. that in principle he broke through the persistent intellectualism of the scholastic theological tradition and once again opened up to men, after it had been for so long a time overgrown with the weedy growth of useless human tradition, the life-refreshing springs of the divine Word, remains hidden from those English readers of Kuyper to whom we must bring our message. I hope therefore that no publisher will prepare a new edition of this book without first having had the text subjected to a competent scrutiny.

This recovery of 'heart' in its biblical meaning is the real ground for Kuyper's positing so sharply the radical antithesis in all theoretical study (science in the sense of 'Wissenschaft') between the scriptural and all unscriptural standpoints and his pushing the demand for an inner reformation of theoretical thought. And this was necessary in order to see clearly that all that life of theory too is religion, is *heart*-service of God.

The Idea of 'Office'

A second theme in Kuyper's thought that I must refer to in the present discussion is his emphasis upon the idea of *office* (ambt). One of the reasons why sphere-sovereignty is not clear to us, I am quite confident, is that we have lost out of our modern consciousness an awareness of the role of *office* in our life.

Modern society with its revolutionary idea of the popular will and of the right of reason to create society as it itself sees fit has grown to be a *levelled* society. Each 'centre of rationality' is equal with every other. In the political world this finds its expression in the concept of an egalitarian democracy, which is simply another way of saying the *vox populi vox Dei* of the French Revolution. And anyone who thinks that such radical ideas do not exist in our lands is due for a rude awakening. I have never forgotten the shock I received when in 1949 I read an article sent from Paris by the editor of a very prominent American newspaper. The French, so I read, were forever complaining that they could not find out what American foreign policy was, and so could not determine how to adjust to it.

The American editor then proceeded to 'explain' that what he tried to make clear to the French was that America really could not in that sense have a foreign policy since its position was constantly being modified in response to the postcards, letters, telegrams, etc. that every day streamed into congressmen's offices from the citizens, who really determine policy.

Any idea of a societal *order* which God has been pleased to govern by a variety of offices remains foreign to modern society. And many, many Christians in reality think every day of their lives in the modern way at this point. Even among us of the Reformed tradition, as we say, there is a general slovenliness in handling matters that express more deeply than words can our loss of the biblical idea of office. In The Netherlands one could often find a formalistic emphasis upon 'office', which is, after all, simply a distortion of revelational truth. But let us not in our reaction against this formalistic error reject the scriptural truth which made the error possible. Let us not here drift — as so much of our life on this continent is a thoughtless drift — into a modern, rationalistic and revolutionary way of looking at our life and society.

'Office' as Service and Administration

The biblical idea of office brings us to the heart of religion. While the word itself scarcely occurs in Scripture, the idea of office is expressed by such terms as 'service', 'servant of the Lord' (Jehovah), etc. Present in the idea are such related concepts as commission or charge or mandate (opdracht) and delegated authority, definite appointment to carry out the mandate. 'Office' speaks of service in the first place, but there is the additional idea of preserving order. Thus office in the Scripture suggests the allocation of a particular task (of service in preserving order) and the bestowing of a particular right to perform it. Such office implies first a Sovereign, One whose absolute right it is to give the command, to make the appointment, to hold responsible and then the delegated sovereignty, the right to act sovereignly in the name of the Sovereign by virtue of His commission. Office means therefore limitation; for the person in office is not himself The Sovereign, but stands under the absolutely sovereign authority. We conclude that office expresses the fact that man is placed to a certain task with a divine calling to perform it. It is the familiar idea of the cultural mandate. How better could one express the scriptural revelation that all our life is religion, a single-hearted service of God in the whole of the creation. For that reason the concept of office is close to that of the fear of the Lord, in fact, to that of faith and of being a child of God.

Office is not merely service (dienen); it is also administration (bedienen): it is service of God and an administering of God's love and solicitude to the creature at the same time. Office as administration (preserving and orderly form-giving) includes the idea that the future weal or woe of what is being administered depends upon whether the office-bearer does or does not serve God. Scripture speaks of a number of such offices that are both service and administration: of prophet, teacher, priest, judge, king, father, husband, etc. The authority of a father over his children does not really lie in his having begotten them but in his having been charged by God himself with that responsibility. This is a divine ordinance. And that is what is meant by office.

Central Rule of Christ and Church-institute

All the offices that thus stand alongside one another in our functional life seem to find their concentration in the office of man as covenant head. And here Kuyper is quite specific. Christ the second Person of the Godhead possesses absolute sovereignty; but to Him as *Mediator* has been *given* complete (delegated) sovereignty. He is *the* full and complete Office-bearer. And because His mediatorial sovereignty is total such total sovereignty is nowhere to be found in our life on earth. Total sovereignty cannot exist in two places. Christ has delegated only partial sovereignties to men. In Christ all these sovereignties are united in an undivided service of God that involves no less than the redemption of all of life. Christ was sent of God into the world; "lo, I come to do thy will, O God", He Himself confesses.

In this way Kuyper arrives at the idea of the *universality of religion* or of life (in its totality) as religion, which makes it possible to see the difference between the institute of the church and the central religious Rule of Christ. As Dr. Von Meyenfeldt writes in a recent book: "Kuyper durft te zeggen, dat 'de eigenlijke strijd tegen Satan geschiedt niet door dit zichtbare instituut, o op verre na niet . . . Die strijd wordt gestreden in de harten, in de huisgezinnen, in de familiën, in de gesprekken, in de publieke opinie, bij handel en nering, in bedrijf en beroep, in wetenschap en kunst, bij wieg en graf, kortom, zover uw menselijk leven strekt, strekt ook die strijd' (*E voto* II, p. 134f.). Bij Kuyper is de wedergeboorte uitgangspunt, de omzetting dus van de persoon, zoals die aan zijn kerkelijk leven vooraf moet gaan. Wedergeboorte valt m.a.w. buiten de actie-radius van het instituut der kerk. Aan de kerk valt slechts de beperkte taak toe van Dienst des Woords en de aankleve van dien."

The office of the church-institute is a limited office: it is the official administration of Word and sacraments. Its office-bearers have a decidedly limited authority. But that Word, though the church as institute carries the responsibility for its faithful proclamation, is Rule for the whole of life, and every other, also limited, administration must each in its delegated sphere and with its bestowed right and responsibility, preserve and give orderly form, according to that Word's light, to the area over which it has been set by the Sovereign and in accordance with the laws that God has put for that sphere. Here in a nutshell is the idea of sphere-sovereignty. Sovereignty in this expression means, as you have seen, *delegated* sovereignty, and also *limited* sovereignty, sovereignty that is limited to a certain sphere. But it carries also the meaning of *coördinate* sovereignties. No delegated and limited sovereignty is *sub*ordinated to any other: each delegation of authority is directly from Christ. Thus, for instance, the husband's authority is not derived from the State of which he is a citizen or subject, but from Christ Himself. (Cf. Eph. 5:23 ff with I Cor. 11:3) Thus all these coördinate services and administrations do not within themselves display relationships of part and whole, but each of them is part, part of that total service of God that is rendered unto God by Jesus Christ as Head and Root of re-born humanity.

Key to Understanding Scripture

With this construction a great mass of biblical data falls into place, not only the limited authority of the king in the Old Testament theocracy (II Chron. 26) but also such apostolic instructions as are given in Ephesians 5:15—6:9. The divine delegation of office in the life of the State is clear from many places in Scripture, especially from what Jesus said to Pilate. And the interesting passage in Psalm 82 relating to the judges in Israel — "I said, Ye are gods . . . nevertheless ye shall die like men" — simply cannot be understood apart from a distinction between the office and the man who holds the office.

It is not my intention to go on presenting biblical evidence on this occasion. The Groen Club syllabus, *The Bible and the Life of the Christian,* was prepared to meet just such a need. The underlying theme of that syllabus is human life as a service of God in accordance with the principle of sphere-sovereignty. You will find plenty of biblical evidence there.

Delineation of State Authority

Kuyper lived at a time when state-absolutism was a risingtide. To that tendency he directed this prophetic word: the State has as much power as God bestows upon it; no more, but also no less. It sins not only by usurping authority but also when it does not make use of all the authority given to it. The power of the state is constantly limited by that of all the other life-spheres. It does not stand by itself, but is only one of the links in the great chain which holds all the Creation intrinsically together. It cannot interfere in that life which properly belongs to another sphere because God has not delegated it competence therefor. The father, for instance, exercises his proper authority also by divine commission, and the government may not enter into that divine arrangement. Government as *office* is an institution of divine origin, quite independently of whether the persons of the government fear God. The grace of God lies in the existence of the governmental authority itself and therefore we must obey it, but only within the God-ordained limits of its powers. Thus the state takes its place not *above* but *alongside* all the other spheres.

Other Illustrations of Sphere-Sovereignty

A nice illustration of sphere-sovereignty is provided by considering what is involved in the completing of a marriage. Marriage, says Kuyper, is a matter for the bride and bridegroom. It is their solemn oaths to each other that is the essential thing.

But, of course, the two families are also involved. And church and state. Neither the state, however, nor the church performs the marriage. But the state regulates the marriage with respect to its civil side and the church with respect to *its* sphere of competence.

The matter of federal aid to education provides us with a second useful illustration. The task of rearing the new generation (of which education is a part) belongs not to the state but to the parents. At this point many Christians might be inclined to deny any involvement of the state in education. Yet the state does have the responsibility of seeing to it that its citizens be sufficiently educated to permit it to continue to compete with other states in international life. If the parents are unable to maintain such an educational process, it is legitimate and proper for the state to provide the extra monies that are needed to secure those educational processes which it as state requires for its own existence. This is not state intervention in the sphere of parental responsibility; here the state is related *as state* to children who at the same time are citizens.

Likewise, the state does not intervene in the parental sphere when it requires a son to go to war. Here the state is functioning as state in a sphere beyond the competence of the father's delegated authority. The difficulty which most people have at this point is that they confuse 'family' with the concrete totality of life-in-the-kitchen. But concrete life is *religion,* and the persons in the kitchen are related to each other in many ways. The son may be business manager of the father. Both are citizens. The mother may be teacher of her daughter at college. Yet in the instituted church both are believers. At the breakfast table we do not have just family, but *religion,* the totality of life in its diversity of offices. Only persons who think of 'family' as concrete and total can declare that the state's summoning of a 'son' to army service is an intervention in the life of the 'family' and proof that sphere-sovereignty does not exist. Rightly understood, we have here a prime example of what Abraham Kuyper meant by sphere-sovereignty.

In the address he delivered on the official opening-day of the Free University, Kuyper used a figure to express his grandiose view of human life. We see, he said, that our human life is neither simple nor uniform, but an infinitely complex organism, so put together that that which is individual exists only in groups, and that only in those groups the whole can be revealed. We might call the parts of this one great machine cogged wheels (the spheres). (I am expanding Kuyper's illustration a bit as I go on.) As this machine is put into motion each wheel turns on its own individual axis (law for the sphere), but the cogs slide into each other as is seen in the gear system of a car. The wheels work upon each other, but do not interfere with each other. If, however, one wheel were of its own accord to extend its circumferential boundary, its cogs would crash into the other cogs and damage the operation of the machine.

From such a standpoint Kuyper could point to the fact that in the past when one life-sphere attempted to interfere in the proper affairs of another — e.g. the government in business or churches in state and vice versa — things did not go well.

Scriptural proof

I am sometimes asked what proof-texts there are for sphere-sovereignty, and the professor of sacred cow fame (see above, p. 139) has repeatedly stoutly declared that there are none. No; there are not, if you want a single verse. But at least the theologians among us know that a similar state of affairs prevails with respect to such a fundamental doctrine as that of the Trinity. Permit me to quote B. B. Warfield here. In the volume of his collected writings entitled *Biblical Doctrines* (p. 143) he writes: "It is not in a text here and there that the New Testament bears its testimony to the doctrine of the Trinity. The whole book is Trinitarian to the core; all its teaching is built on the assumption of the Trinity; and its allusions to the Trinity are frequent, cursory, easy and confident. It is with a view to the cursoriness of the allusions to it in the New Testament that it has been remarked that 'the doctrine of the Trinity is not so much heard as overheard in the statements of Scripture'". In like manner I would say of sphere-sovereignty that its biblical proof is the integral meaning of scriptural revelation; without sphere-sovereignty the Scriptures simply cannot be understood.

Not Cut and Dried

That does not mean, of course, that every detail in connection with sphere-sovereignty is crystal clear; for it is not.

Several troublesome ambiguities in Kuyper's own thought on the matter have been cleared up since his time. Some of you now listening to me may be able to pose some difficulties. I shall try to meet them — if not in the paper then in the discussion afterwards.

The general *fact* of sphere-sovereignty ought, however, to be clear from the foregoing. If all the constantly changing states of affairs (functional processes) of the positivist can nevertheless be shown to be of a *variety of kinds* — e.g. physical-chemical biotic, psychical, analytical — *that are irreducible,* i.e. maintain their distinct identity, *and* further *display an invariable order of time* — e.g. 'the biotic' necessarily presupposing 'the physical-chemical' as 'earlier"; the psychical, the biotic —; if only to Christ as Mediator is given all-authority, the diversity of delegated and modally limited 'authorities' in our human life being a coördinate diversity within that all-authority; if the Kingdom of God is the whole of re-directed human life, the diversity of spheres in our life being so many coördinate aspects of that fulness of life; — if these things are so, then sphere-sovereignty is indeed the expression of the very constitution of the whole creation-order, and our knowledge of it — a *religious* or heart knowledge, acquired when through the Power of the Word of God we 'see' or 'know' Christ and His Kingdom —, is the Directing Principle of our life in the world.

A Difficulty

One preliminary difficulty that may possibly — and with good reason — have announced itself to your mind I should like to discuss here. If sphere-sovereignty is as eminently scriptural, as intimately bound up with the whole structure of the divine word-revelation, as has been proposed here this morning, then how does it happen that knowledge of it did not appear on the scene until Kuyper? This is, as I said, a justified question. Although to give an answer to it will take a little time, the resulting increased insight into the significance of sphere-sovereignty will amply reward us. Of course, we shall have to be brief, but I will refer you to the literature.

Before Kuyper

In one sense we can certainly say that the theme of sphere-sovereignty did not first appear in Kuyper. Dr. J. D. Dengerink, in his important book *Critisch-Historisch Onderzoek naar de Sociologische Ontwikkeling van het Beginsel der "Souvereiniteit in Eigen Kring" in de 19e en 20e Eeuw*, discusses in this connection two men of the generation immediately preceding Kuyper's, viz. the great German Lutheran statesman and philosopher, Dr. Friedrich Julius Stahl, and the founder of the Dutch Christian political movement, Guillaume Groen van Prinsterer, both of them influenced by the Reveil-movement, the revival of Christian belief in Switzerland, to which Robert Haldane of Scotland also contributed of his knowledge of the Word of God by discussing the book of Romans with the — largely Unitarian — theological students in Geneva. (See J. C. Rullmann, *De Afscheiding*.)

Stahl

Stahl's writings show points of contact for the scriptural idea of sphere-sovereignty. As long as he speaks in the context of the Word of God he shows evidence of an insight into the distinct natures and the independent significance of the several spheres of society. In particular, Stahl sees a guarantee for the existence of independent spheres in the fact that the government is bound to the divine world-order. He sees as such independent spheres the church in the first place, but also the state and marriage. Sometimes — for example, in his struggle against socialism — he even shows an insight into the independent significance of industry. In spite of all this, however, another view of society dominates in his thinking, viz. that of the historism of the German Historical School.

Guillaume Groen van Prinsterer

Groen van Prinsterer was influenced by Stahl especially in his view of the state, but he gradually became a Calvinist, and thus emphasized much more than Stahl did the lawful character of the world. For him Scripture had a much more direct significance for our functional life in this world. Whereas the Lutheran dualism is felt in Stahl, in Groen we see that the Bible is the infallible divine word-revelation which provides the foundation for law and morals, authority and freedom. Nevertheless, the same historistic view that dominates in Stahl came to play a large role in his thinking too, in the first place because he had not yet seen that the word-revelation was meant to produce an *inner* reformation of all of life.

For Groen the Word of God provides for our functional life only the *limits within which human culture has freedom to develop*. Even our science remains for him a more or less autonomous source of knowledge for the truth, and upon it no higher demand is put than that it *not come into conflict* with the express pronouncements of Holy Scripture. Within the limits set by Scripture (as he understands it) the historism of his age comes to influence his view of society. History retains for him a relative autonomy with respect to the divine word-revelation. Of necessity this means that his view of history comes to be governed by another religious ground-motive than that of Holy Scripture. Groen has not yet clearly seen at this point the role of the Word of God in our lives, nor, consequently, the intrinsic connection that exists between that Word and the living of our lives — including our theoretical lives — in the world.

The then current Historical School of thought led both Stahl and Groen to accept, in reaction against the Enlightenment, a view of society in which the independence of the various 'spheres', *with the important exception of the church-institute,* is conceived as an autonomy, within the totality of the State, of subordinate parts that have acquired rights of existence in the course of historical development.

About this view I wish at this point to make two remarks. First, that such a view provides at most only a *relative* guarantee of the independence of the various spheres. For what — except the will to be a conservative! (but who wishes to keep *all* historical growths?) — gives the right to call a halt to historical change at any particular stage of it? And as *parts* of the State what gives the other spheres any ultimate independence from the State? But even more important, in the second place, is the consideration that by taking historically acquired rights as their criterion of independence these men had no satisfactory way of judging what are really independent spheres.

Both Stahl and Groen excluded the church, as I have intimated, from their generally historistic view of society. This, as I hope will become clearer in a few minutes, was due to the traditional power of the ground-motive of nature and grace, which had dominated thought among Christians about church and state in most periods of the church's history, and took hold of Reformation groups in the Protestant scholasticism that so quickly succeeded upon the first glorious effort at Reformation in the 16th century.

Kuyper

Now we can see that Abraham Kuyper marks a great advance beyond his predecessors. For he clearly grasped the principle of sphere-sovereignty in its universal cosmic significance, and grounded it explicitly, in the scriptural sense, in the Order of creation. That is, he saw it as *creation-principle*. But even with Kuyper this was more an intuitive insight than a carefully worked out analysis. He lacked an intrinsically Christian philosophical view of reality, and this, in turn, gave rise to a number of serious ambiguities in his thought. Moreover, in Kuyper too, historism and the traditional ground-motive of nature and grace play a noticeable role, especially in his works *Anti-revolutionaire Staatkunde* and *Ons Program*.

You will remember that in this section of my lecture I am attempting to explain how it was that an awareness of the scriptural principle of sphere-sovereignty did not arise until the second half of the nineteenth century. Following the study made by Dr. Dengerink I have indicated that before Kuyper, in Stahl and even more in Groen, there was *some* acknowledgement of what we have later come to know as sphere-sovereignty. Where these men were following closely the thought of Scripture, traces of a developing statement of this creation-principle can be detected. But any full maturation of the idea was held in check by the current Historical School, with its view of societal development, and by the more traditional ground-motive of nature and grace. Even in Kuyper, who first consciously articulated the principle of sphere-sovereignty, a consistent elaboration of it was hampered by the opposing influence of the same two factors. In him too we can clearly see a principle derived from scriptural reflection struggling to take on historical form, but hindered by powerful historical forces already long at work that proceed from an opposing principle.

To be able to point to two men in the generation immediately preceding that of Kuyper is, in itself, not much historical evidence, at least not in the quantitative sense. But we are, I believe, beginning to see something. We must remember that from the middle of the 17th century until the Reveil of the early 19th the Protestant movement had largely fallen before the onslaughts of the secularist movement that dominates our modern centuries. With the Reveil came a renewed knowledge of Scripture, and then at once we begin to see the powerful influence of that Word, and then more and more, in the thought of men like Stahl and Groen and Kuyper. When these men deal with fresh problems in the more immediate light of the divine Word, a distinct principle of societal order begins to come to expression; when they work in more traditional areas and with the traditional or more current humanistic concepts, another principle is felt to be at work. There is struggle here, the struggle to be reformed according to the Word of God from those other (pseudo-)principles that had taken a firm hold on men's hearts and darkened human understanding.

Time of the Reformation

And now I wish to introduce one further piece of historical evidence; for it will serve to strengthen the conviction we have just arrived at. If it is a return to the Word of God that stimulates an expression of the principle of sphere-sovereignty, then why do we not hear of this principle at the time of the mighty Reformation of the 16th century? The fact is that we do.

Althusius

In recent years Prof. H. Dooyeweerd, dean of the faculty of law at the Free University of Amsterdam, has repeatedly called our attention to the thought of the Calvinistic legal theorist of Herborn, Johannes Althusius (a younger contemporary of Jean Bodin), who in the early years of the 17th century and over against Bodin's ideas of state-absolutism developed a structural theory with regard to human society which was built on an acknowledgement of a divine world-order and the inner nature of the societal spheres. In this theory Althusius pointed out that each of these spheres has its own law, proper to its nature, and its own sphere of authority, which is not to be derived from any other. (See Dooyeweerd, *De Crisis der Humanistische Staatsleer*, p. 147 f. and the literature there referred to; *A New Critique of Theoretical Thought*

III, p. 662 f.; *De Christelijke Staatsidee,* p. 28 f.; *De Strijd om het Souvereiniteitsbegrip in de Moderne Rechts- en Staatsleer,* p. 21 f.)

Unfortunately, the great Berlin professor of law, Otto von Gierke, in his *Johannes Althusius und die Entwicklung der naturrechtlichen Staatstheorien* (4th ed. Breslau, 1929; Engl. tr. in Gierke, *Development of Political Theory,* N.Y., 1939), and also in his monumental study *Das deutsche Genossenschaftsrecht* (an English translation of a large part of the fourth volume of which can now easily be procured in the Beacon paperback edition, entitled *Natural Law and the Theory of Society,* 1500-1800), and Gierke's pupil, Waldecker, misinterpreted Althusius' organic view of symbiosis, taking it in the biological sense; these men related his doctrine to the (later) secular theory of natural law, with its concept of the social contract and its idea of state-absolutism *à la* the romantic deist Rousseau. In this way the biblical principle of sphere-sovereignty, arising out of the integral reflection of the (Calvinistic) Reformation, has been hidden from our view because the great humanist scholars of our history-conscious 19th and 20th centuries seem generally unable to enter understandingly into modes of thought so very divergent from the big lines of humanistic development. (Here is an important reason why the A.R.S.S. should quickly erect a Centre for Higher Studies on a Reformed — i.e. radically and integrally scriptural — Basis.)

Even in Germany, however, there is a beginning of recognition of misinterpretation. Dooyeweerd has referred, for example, to the work *Verfassungslehre* by C. Schmitt (1928), p. 77: "Das *Volk* hat bei Althusius schon eine potestas *constituta.* Die Säkularisierung des Begriffes der konstituierenden Gewalt tritt erst später ein. Auf keinem Fall darf man hier, wie Gierke in seinem berühmten Werk über Althusius die Begriffe eines gläubigen Calvinisten wie Althusius mit denen eines romantischen Deisten wie Rousseau zusammenbringen." But here is not the place to go more deeply into this matter.

Calvin

If I may be permitted just one more step back into history, I should like to suggest that Calvin himself had, from his recovered knowledge of the centrality and totality of the Christian religion, come to some grasp of sphere-sovereignty as the basic principle of cosmic order. The important passage here is *Institutes* IV

11. 1: "For as no city or town can exist without a magistracy and civil polity, so the Church of God . . . stands in need of a certain spiritual polity."

It is true that Calvin seems generally to have had an eye only for the two magnitudes of church and state, so that we can scarcely speak here of sphere-sovereignty in the more elaborated sense in which we have come to think of it since Kuyper. Nevertheless, this passage contains the scriptural idea that the church-institute does not at all exhaust the richness of the Kingdom of God among men, and that in essence the church does not occupy a place *above* all other societal relationships.

Moreover, the late Prof. Josef Bohatec, the historian of the University of Vienna who was undoubtedly most at home, of all men of our time, in the sources for Calvin's life and work, and who, in his standard work *Calvins Lehre von Staat und Kirche* (1937), demonstrated the weaknesses in Ernst Troeltsch's treatment *(Die Soziallehren der christlichen Kirchen und Kirchengruppen)* of the social ideas of Calvin and the other reformers, this Prof. Bohatec — a man, by the way, who, while he lived, was a most ardent supporter of the movement for an intrinsically Christian philosophy — says, in articles he wrote for the periodical *Antirevolutionaire Staatkunde* (1926) on "De Organische Idee in de Gedachtenwereld van Calvijn", that although modern scholars are somewhat aware of the Calvinistic view that human society forms an organic unity, i.e. a structure of ordinances which the sovereign God has given to the creation, they have paid little attention to the idea of an organic society in Calvin. That is primarily due to the fact that they have directed their attention almost solely to his doctrine of the church. (You see that we need more scholars than just theologians!) Bohatec distinguishes Calvin's thought from the medieval idea of *corpus christianum* and shows that Calvin's objection to both a world-church and a world-state is this, that not only can neither bring to realization the organic unity that is aimed at but they both bring about disorganization and tyranny. Bohatec proceeds to show that, having rejected both extreme forms of development, Calvin attempts to bring both typical regulations of life into one organic whole. In this he wished to bring out, according to Bohatec, that both, each in its own sphere, must claim independence since as arrangements or regulations (ordeningen) put by God they have to be *of equal value*. The full significance of this observation can only be felt when we compare Calvin's view with the traditional view of his time as to the relation between church and state.

Basic Reason for Late Emergence of Sphere-Sovereignty

We have now seen that not only in the revival of scripturally directed life and thinking in the 19th century but also in the Reformation of the sixteenth sphere-sovereignty insinuated itself into human thinking. That it did not become more widely accepted and better known is due to the fact that the energies of the Reformation movement were early dissipated and that the Christian revival of the early 19th century was not only limited in its sphere of influence but also checked by its accommodating itself to traditional and current ways of thinking about society.

The failure of the idea of sphere-sovereignty to come into its own was first of all due to the fact that by the time of the Reformation the Christian Church had for long centuries — actually from the early days of the church fathers (*patres,* patristic age), and in the time of the medieval scholastics — accommodated itself to an imposing edifice of theoretical construction with regard to the state that makes sphere-sovereignty an impossibility. The newly won intellectual converts of the early patristic centuries had, before their conversion, been steeped in that pagan tradition of an all-embracing state-power.

Classical View of the State

Emerging from an undifferentiated form of society (see Dooyeweerd, *A New Critique* III and Index *sub voce* undifferentiated), the Greek people had developed a differentiated form in which the state or political power came to assume the place of the all-embracing association in which all other forms of human association are included as parts within the whole. You are, I am sure, acquainted with the Greek conception of the *polis* or city-state. This was, from the scriptural view of sphere-sovereignty, a fundamentally distorted conception, a fundamentally misdirected way of life. Any insight into the central Kingdom-rule of Christ being lacking, one of the many spheres of our functional life had become enlarged, blown up far beyond its *proper* sphere — the sphere for which Christ has delegated to its offices His sovereign power — and been made the absolute and ultimate authority.

The seeds of totalitarianism do not lie in certain developments of the 19th century; they are *intrinsic to unbiblical thought* and are found at the very beginning of western political theory. It is this that we still see in the Historical School of the time of Stahl and Groen. Even though other spheres of human life be granted a certain autonomy on the principle of hoary antiquity and acquired rights, as subordinate *parts* of the political whole these spheres have no basically guaranteed independence; for the part is governed ultimately by the same authority as the whole. The Historical School has not saved us from the levelling and totalitarian tendencies of the Enlightenment.

When the Gospel and the Church came into the Roman world, they found already there a mammoth state-organization, which was giving increasingly clear expression to its *religious* character in the encouragement of emperor-worship: the *imperium Romanum*. Here again the state or political power was the totality, of which marriage, family, etc. were the subordinate parts. The state was thus the *societas perfecta;* all other forms of association were *societas imperfectae*. The emperor was the bearer of the totalitarian authority of the old Greek and Roman heads of state. He was not looked upon as office-bearer in one of life's spheres, which, together with all other spheres — including that of the instituted church —, makes up the central religious Rule of Christ in His Kingdom of Righteousness (i.e. the Kingdom where everything is 'right' according to the demands of the creation ordinances), thus exhibiting the *religious* nature of reality.

Thus when a Christian living in the Roman Empire referred to the state he was on the one hand speaking about one kind of human association that is grounded in the creation-order, but on the other only able to point to it as an historical actuality in the distorted form that arises from apostate religion.

The 'Christian' Accommodation

When the Fathers of the Church were confronted with the necessity of relating the new society, the Church, to the state as it existed for them in the Roman Empire, they did not, from a scriptural sense of the structure of reality, re-form or attempt to reform their state, but rather largely accepted it as it had gradually developed in the historical experience of the classical peoples. Leaving the whole world of interpretation of life and society that was embedded in that (distorted) institution essentially untouched and un-reformed by the quickening word-revelation of God, they sought a solution by thinking of the Church as an *addition* to that civil society.

To use the language of our modern positivistically-minded opponents of sphere-sovereignty, *they stayed with the 'facts'* (i.e. adjusted to what was there all about them). But in doing so, let us be sure to observe, *they lost hold of the FACTS*. For in every positive 'fact' of human society there is not only some inescapable *structure of the creation ordinances* (e.g. one cannot set up a form of the state that is not somehow bound to the structural requirements of state), but also the *degree of conformity to or deviation from the creation-norm* (which is a command, a norm; not a structural law in the sense of natural laws) that was operative in the cultural forming-activity of the men who 'built' the *polis*, built Rome. When a man's eyes are closed to this fact, whether he be fourth-century church father or twentieth-century positivistic professor, he is, in a very important sense, blind to the integral meaning of the Scriptures, and without their light he will not be in a position to see any social fact for what it is. If men wish to call such blindness sticking to the facts, well and good, provided we all know that 'sticking to the facts' means that kind of blindness.

Hinc Illae Lacrimae

By doing what they did the church fathers did not solve their difficulties but only brought a new rash of trouble over our already burdened human race. By conceiving the Church as a society additional to civil society, and by failing to distinguish Church as the Body of Christ from the church as (cultic) institute they had themselves introduced into western society a *second* totalitarian association. For the Rule of Christ *is* total; the Kingdom of God is the *total renewal, in Christ, of life in all its structures*. Yet the officers of the church-institute possess no such total authority. Frightful tensions, fundamental rifts in authority, had to result. In this way the unity of all spheres of life as aspects of a central service of God in the Rule of Christ could not be achieved.

As Body of Christ the Church would have to effect a reformation (also) of the paganistically distorted structure of the state. (See Col. 1:20 and the *Korte Verklaring* on this passage.) Christians "instinctively" — i.e. religiously — felt this; so too did the popes. And the claim of the popes to be Vicar of Christ on earth assumed a more totalitarian authority than is granted to the office-bearers of the church-institute. But we must always remember in this connection that Kingdom or City of God and church-institute were confused in their minds.

On the other hand, the totalitarian state, as that had developed, could permit no encroachment upon its (total) authority. Here is the origin of the struggle between Emperor and Pope, between State and Church. The problem is still with us, and in the form it has assumed it can never be resolved. For though the state *is* independent of the church-institute, and vice-versa (since both are modally limited authorities in the Kingdom of God), a really *totalitarian* state (the concept of the classical peoples, of the Enlightenment and, essentially, of the Historical School of jurisprudence) and the *central religious claim of Christ* cannot be reconciled. (The American debate about the first article of the Bill of Rights of our Constitution.) Here we have the root-struggle between true and false religion, what we know as The Antithesis, that conflict which God graciously introduced into our history when He established the Church.

Once the Church had accepted a "natural" realm of civil polity as a concrete area of life not needing to be re-formed by the living Word of God, not only was a foothold given to the rebellious (revolutionary) mind of apostasy, in the form of a totalitarian state, to wage war upon the people of Christ, but, in addition, the Church was compelled to conceive of itself *in a reduced way* as *another* concrete area (the *supra*-natural one) *alongside*, i.e. above the *"natural"*.

Thus the traditional 'Christian' "solution" of church fathers and medieval scholastics was no real solution. It allowed a false form of state by denying as a matter of principle that it needed to be reformed according to the Truth of the divine word-revelation. At the same time it introduced the false notion of a limited (to the supranatural 'area') Rule of Christ through His Word. This having been done, neither state nor church-institute (nor either, for that matter, the central religious Rule of Christ) could be seen for what they *are* according to the constitutive Will of God. These facts cannot be seen until we have abandoned the so-called positive (i.e. not normed) 'facts' of positivist theory and, illumined in the depth-level of our hearts by the Word, been brought to 'see' the religious root of our temporal existence. You will do well to read what Prof. Dooyeweerd has written about this in his standard work, *A New Critique of Theoretical Thought* III, 214-222.

In such a Christian thinker as Augustine there is to be seen the conflict between conceiving state and church as natural and supranatural entities and conceiving the *civitas Dei* as the total re-creation of life in all its complexity. There is on the one hand the attempted *accommodation* (synthesis) of the light of the Word of God to the ancient understanding of what the state is; on the other, a real grasping of what God teaches about the central religious authority of Christ the Mediator.

It is this fundamental conflict which Christians have inherited from the beginning of the New Testament church that explains the slow conquest in Christians' hearts of the scriptural teaching about sphere-sovereignty. Let no one here underestimate the historical forming-power of a long tradition. Attachment to the traditional theory resulted in the *suppression* of the creation-motive of the Christian religion in the Christians' view of reality. It is the slow victory of the Word of God over a powerful accommodation theory that we feel in the work of Calvin, of Althusius, of Stahl, Groen and even Kuyper.

Sphere-Sovereignty From Scriptural Ground-motive

We have now seen enough to understand a very significant word of Dr. Dengerink's in his book on sphere-sovereignty. On p. 162 he writes: (In the preceding) "it proved repeatedly that the principle of sphere-sovereignty pressed itself upon the several Christian writers as long as the Scriptural motive of creation maintained its hold upon their thought, but that in the actual sociological elaboration they again came under the influence to a greater or lesser extent of universalistic conceptions, of either a scholastic or a modern-historistic origin. At the same time, the synthesis motive of Nature and Grace proved to be responsible, in the last analysis, for the departure from the Scriptural line."

The above I offer in reply to the question how it could come about that a theme so intimately bound up with the heart of the Gospel had to wait so long for explicit acknowledgement.

Recent Clarification

In conclusion I should like to quote one more paragraph from the book of Dengerink. He continues: "With Kuyper reformational thought was seen to have arrived at a critical juncture, since he more sharply than any of his predecessors saw the radical antithesis in scholarship between a Scriptural and an unscriptural standpoint and posited the demand of an inner reformation of scientific thought. It was he who first grasped the meaning of the principle of sphere-sovereignty in its cosmological significance and creational foundation . . . . However, a scientific-sociological working out of this principle proved to be impossible without a philosophical theory of reality rooted in divine Word revelation. Having grasped this principle is the real significance of the founders of modern Calvinist philosophy. In particular the professors Vollenhoven and Dooyeweerd have been trail blazers."

In Abraham Kuyper, in spite of his intuitive grasp of the cosmic principle of sphere-sovereignty, there is still much of the idea of an *autonomy* of spheres on the basis of historically acquired rights. But this idea of the Historical School offered no genuine criterion for a sphere. What is a sphere? Kuyper could not really answer this question adequately, because he lacked, as Dengerink writes, a philosophical theory of reality that is truly intrinsically fructified by the divine word-revelation. The contemporary philosophical school of the Free University of Amsterdam saw this need, and its theory of the modal scale and of the structures of individuality attempts to provide an answer. I cannot on this occasion go into it any more than I have in the preceding. Suffice it to say that a proper understanding of this theory removes the objection that the spheres overlap. Think of what I wrote about the family around the breakfast table. Prof. Dooyeweerd's theory has enabled him also to work out a much more precise theory about the *positive* task of the state.

* * *

We have come a long way since I raised the question whether

we may *accept* the fact of an industrial society, and whether we possess anywhere such an insight, such a directing Principle, as will enable us to work in the immediate situations of our complex and disordered society to re-form and restore it to the Order of the divine creation-ordinance. My answer is that God has given us a Principle by which we can 'see' to do our work. Sphere-sovereignty is an eminently *evangelical* principle: it is given with the Gospel itself. This must be our Christian answer to all the Bertrand Russells and their nihilism.

The world cries out its need of a directing Principle. We, by the grace of God, are the "blessed possessors". Men who have discovered such pure gold can never belong to a Silent Generation, who have no Cause to strive for. With a proper understanding of sphere-sovereignty we are, in Christ, more than conquerors, more than the equals, for example, of the communists, whose Karl Marx once said that while philosophy had hitherto confined itself to interpreting the world, the point was to *change* it. For communism, lacking the Gospel, misses the directing Principle of our life. How then can it know that its changes are in the good direction? As a matter of fact, it is well known that also the communist world is plagued by a *pragmatic drift*. But to His people God has revealed the Principle for the direction of life.

I can do no better than to end with those beautiful words that Prof. Van Riessen wrote in *The Society of the Future* (p. 230): "Principles are a creation-mandate; they come as such to man in the way of redemption in Christ, and their function is that emancipation of life, with respect to its societal forms, which is intended in that redemption and is first made possible by it. They are links in the chain of redemption, and they only function properly when the man who manipulates them is filled with a truly Christian spirit. Then they become manifestations of that love of the neighbour which is only genuinely possible when it proceeds from the *great* commandment. Then they become manifestations of respect not for man but for the *calling* of man and thus also for the room he needs to pursue that calling and to give a *direct accounting* of his life and works; in sum, respect for life as *Gottesdienst*." Let us forever be thankful that all our life *may* be religion.

There is no evangelical theme that is more in need of a forceful, relevant interpretation and application to the world of our time than this one of sphere-sovereignty, which you have so patiently listened to me unfold here this morning. With Prof. Van Riessen I believe, "it is here that the decisive battle will be fought against totalitarianism and for a christian society." (p. 73).

Literature: In addition to the literature listed at the end of the second chapter of the Groen Club syllabus, *The Bible and the Life of the Christian* (now published by The Presbyterian and Reformed Publishing Company) I would mention:

1) art. J. D. Dengerink, "Das Wort Gottes und die zeitlichen sozialen Ordnungen", in *Philosophia Reformata,* Vol. 20 (1955), pp. 97-122;

2) art. J. D. Dengerink, "Ordening van het maatschappelijk leven", in *Antirevolutionaire Staatkunde,* Vol. 30, no. 12 (Dec. 1960), pp. 332-354.

TOMORROWS BOOK CLUB

Tomorrow's Book Club (TBC) was organized in 1968 to facilitate the distribution of Christian literature, especially for students. It offers a discount on most of its listings to members who pay an annual membership fee of $2.50. TBC became a subsidiary of Wedge Publishing Foundation in 1970. Recently it purchased the entire stock of the books published earlier by the Association for the Advancement of Christian Scholarship in the Christian Perspectives series. Some of its present listings are:

A. H. De Graaff and C. G. Seerveld,
Understanding the Scriptures:
How to Read and Not to Read the Bible,
$1.65.

H. Hart,
The Challenge of our Age
$2.00.

H. E. Runner,
The Relation of the Bible to Learning,
third edition, $2.50.

P. G. Schrotenboer,
Motives of Ecumenism,
$1.25.

P. Schouls,
Man in Communication,
$1.50.

C. G. Seerveld,
A Christian Critique of Art and Literature,
$1.75.

J. Vander Hoeven,
The Rise and Development of the Phenomenological Movement,
$1.25.

H. Van der Laan,
A Christian Appreciation of Physical Science,
$1.25.

M. Vrieze,
The Community Idea in Canada,
$1.25.

★

TOMORROW'S BOOK CLUB
Post Office Box 10, Station L
Toronto 10, Ontario, Canada